Thinking
Outside
the Book

A VOLUME IN THE SERIES

Studies in Print Culture and the History of the Book

Thinking Outside the Book

AUGUSTA ROHRBACH

University of Massachusetts Press
Amherst and Boston

Printed in the United States of America

ISBN 978-1-62534-126-6 (pbk) 125-9 (cloth)

Designed by Sally Nichols
Set in Monotype Bell
Printed and bound by Sheridan Books, Inc.

Library of Congress Cataloging-in-Publication Data

Rohrbach, Augusta, 1961–
Thinking outside the book / Augusta Rohrbach.
pages cm. — (Studies in print culture and the history of the book)
Includes bibliographical references and index.
ISBN 978-1-62534-125-9 (hardcover : alk. paper) — ISBN 978-1-62534-126-6 (paper : alk. paper) 1. American literature—Women authors—History and criticism. 2. American literature—19th century—History and criticism. 3. Women authors, American—19th century—Political and social views. 4. Authorship—Social aspects—United States—History—19th century. 5. Authors and publishers—United States—History—19th century. 6. Authors and readers—United States—History—19th century. 7. Transmission of texts. 8. Books—History. 9. Books and reading—History. I. Title.
PS149.R64 2014
810.9'928709034—dc23

2014019828

British Library Cataloguing-in-Publication Data
A catalogue record for this book is available from the British Library.

For Larry, Margalit, and Zelda—with love and hope

The book on which I had so much relied; the book in the morocco cover; the book with the cock-hat corners; the book full of fine old family associations; the book with seventeen plates, executed in the highest style of art; this previous book was next to useless. Yes, the thing that had guided the father, could not guide the son. And I sat down on a shop step, and gave loose to meditation.

—Herman Melville, *Redburn* (1849)

Contents

Acknowledgments

I began this book while on a joint appointment at the W. E. B. Du Bois Research Institute and the Radcliffe Institute for Advanced Research (2000–2001). Back then it was called "That Damned Mob of Scribbling Women"—after Hawthorne's scornful remark—and was focused on the ways women write themselves into a marketplace dominated by white male writers. I continued shaping it through my years on the job market, during temporary appointments at Harvard and as the Charles Watts Professor of Book History at Brown. The work took a decided turn for the better when I had the good fortune to be hired to a tenured position at Washington State University and began my editorship of *ESQ*.

At WSU, I was awarded a Meyer project grant in 2007 and then the Buchanan Professorship (2012–2014). Both of these funded research trips and production costs. The Sophia Smith Collection at Smith College supported my work on Sojourner Truth, and the Boston Athenaeum opened its doors to me as I worked on material pertaining to Augusta Evans. I spent a delightful week in Columbia, South Carolina, reviewing Mary Chesnut's manuscripts, and Todd Hagstette helped me, after I left, by transcribing material I found there. Since then, the project developed significantly, as reflected in the publication of several essays—all drawing on subject matter of the book, and each benefiting from the wisdom of editors and readers. But the thing that has most radically changed this book—and my thinking—is the rise of the Internet and the impact of digital technology on how we read, research, and think. Julie Meloni—then a Ph.D. student at WSU—helped me wade into these waters by asking me to work with her on an independent study. The students in my later seminars, especially those who participated in "Introduction to Book History" in 2008 and "Literary History Becoming Digital" in the Fall of 2011, brought their curiosity, goodwill, and imagination to the work we did.

Like so many long-term projects, this one took several important detours along the way, all of which proved formative in part for the gentle and gracious guides that have been indispensable companions, champions, and oft-consulted critics. I am grateful to Lawrence Buell, Melissa Homestead, Henry Louis Gates Jr., Ellen Gruber Garvey, Hollis Robbins, Martha Nell Smith, Robert Dale Parker, Bethany Schneider, John Stauffer, Timothy Patrick McCarthy, Chris Castiglia, Donna Campbell, Joan Burbick, Stephanie Foote, Cynthia Davis, Leon Jackson, Claudia Stokes, Rachael Steinitz, and Arlene Keizer for their questions, feedback, and much-needed caution. Hollis Robbins, in particular, helped me see the path my argument was obscuring, and showed me the way at a crucial juncture in chapter 3. Her remarks embodied all the best that the profession has to offer; she remained unselfish and focused on the ideas.

I am also grateful to all those who have trusted me with their work by submitting to *ESQ*. It is a singular privilege to spend each day learning from other people's ideas, and to have my teachers be the accomplished writers and scholars whose work I come in contact with at the journal. I am also the grateful beneficiary of the seasoned responses provided by those who graciously review manuscripts for the journal, either as board members or as the less recognized but just as essential second reader. Their reports act as models of scholarly communication, imbued as they are with a keen sense of what brings us all to the humanities in general and to literary studies in particular: the power of the word and its enduring value.

It had long been my wish to be a part of the Studies in Print Culture and the History of the Book series at University of Massachusetts Press, begun under the sponsoring editorship of Paul Wright and inaugurated with David Hall's iconic *Cultures of Print.* It has now become a dream fulfilled, made possible by the collective vision of the advisory board, Greg Barnhisel, Robert A. Gross, Joan Shelley Rubin, and Michael Winship. The manuscript had the benefit of the careful attention of several manuscript reviewers, whose suggestions improved the project in so many ways. I cannot offer praise enough for Brian Halley, Carol Betsch, and Mary Bellino—a spectacular team. Special thanks are due to Amanda Heller for her careful (and patient!) work on the manuscript during the editing phase. And many more thanks to the readers for the press who took the time to offer constructive criticism based on the value they saw in the ideas and who were gracious enough to put aside some of the manuscript's deficiencies. The detailed reports they provided are exemplars of the highest professional standards. Together, from readers to editor and copyeditor, they have done much to improve the quality of this project.

Of the friends who have not just endured the duration of this project but enriched it, I am ever in awe of Ravit Reichman, Laura Saltz, Lisa Herschbach, Sam Chang, Aimee Phan, and Howard Horwitz. There are still several more who have replenished my spirit and helped me gather the force I needed to stay with the ideas even when I most wanted to forget them. For their patience, wit, wisdom, and mental toughness, I rely on Will Hamlin and Priscilla Wald through thick and thin. But none of this would be possible without the light Larry Mayer, Margalit, and Zelda shine on me every day.

I have lost several along the way whose love and spirit have imbued this project—and more, this writer. Thank you, Herbert John Rohrbach Jr., Laura May Grayson, J. Gordan Grayson, and the heroic Ed Mayer. Your lessons will be with me always.

Thinking Outside the Book

Introduction

In 2009 the MacArthur Foundation commissioned a group of media and education scholars to study the impact of digital culture on educational practices and outcomes. The executive summary of their report begins with a statistic: "According to a recent study from the Pew Internet & American Life project . . . , more than one-half of all teens have created media content, and roughly one-third of teens who use the Internet have shared content they produced."[1] These statistics have a dramatic bearing on the cultural history and function of publication, for they reveal how the opportunities created by new media allow writers (and readers) to blow by the publishing gatekeepers who have shaped literary history to date, in effect creating a whole generation who think outside the book.

As exciting as these changes may be, they have also generated concerns over their impact not just on our literature but on our culture, past, present, and future. In particular, the publishing opportunities made possible by the technological advances of Web 2.0 exert enormous pressure on the book, as both material fact and cultural form. From the pages of the *New York Times* to the shelves of academic libraries, scholars, cultural critics, and lay readers alike express an intense anxiety over the future—or lack thereof—of the book. This apprehension is not simply about the material artifact we understand as a "book"; rather, it reflects a profound unease about the fate of what the book embodies, namely, the cultural traditions, ritual practices, and other key features that constitute the human experience.[2] And, as the MacArthur-commissioned report on digital media and literacy makes clear, concern over the book quickly translates into concern over broader issues in education and the transmission of culture.

Seldom do literary histories take a crisis in education as their starting point, but *Thinking Outside the Book* does. The massive shift created by advances in Web technology crucially reframes the central terms of book history and the way we teach the field. Once-stable concepts like literacy, authorship, publication, edition, and editor are precisely the categories that new media developments radically challenge. The authors of the MacArthur study offer a useful bridge between the old and the new by insisting that we remain focused on the human aspects of both technology and literacy, arguing that "new media literacies developed through collaboration and networking" are not about technology and our interface therewith, but more profoundly about our interface with one another.[3] This emphasis on participation over interactivity puts people ahead of machines, maintaining a distinction between culture and technology that is especially compelling for humanists.[4] It also harkens back to earlier—but just as radical—alterations in energy around the media we create, consume, and critique.

During the nineteenth century, burgeoning rates of literacy and advances in print technology created the possibility for an American literary culture as vibrant—and as viral—as today's Internet-enabled, Web-based digital context.[5] Looking back to nineteenth-century American literary culture and forward to our contemporary context provides a useful parallax from which to reassess the discipline of literary studies and its place in a future in which our idea of the book has been transformed by new media, that is, a future that will be less and less about the "book" as "a reflection upon action" and more and more about "text" as a form of action itself—posting, blogging, texting, tweeting.[6] Strictly speaking, the term "parallax" refers to a method of measuring distances through an angle of vision that takes in two lines of sight, creating a new perspective.[7] The parallactic view of literary studies yielded by bringing nineteenth-century U.S. literary culture into contact with twenty-first-century new media exposes important synergies while also suggesting useful amendments to the way we think about both sides of this timeline. Among the most useful modifications *Thinking Outside the Book* provides is a new vocabulary, one that promises to generate a method of thinking about literary history—both then and now—that emphasizes the performative over the structural.[8]

My goal in articulating a theory of how literary history is made is not to replace previous work in the field, a large part of which remains crucial to understanding the contributions that literary culture and its study make to a civil society, but rather to mobilize it. So much of the work we do as academics is based on a competitive model of what Kathleen Fitzpatrick called "planned obsolescence."[9] And yet there are a few key concepts that have remained all too stable, among them Literacy, Authorship, Publication, Edition, and Editor. Although each of these building blocks of print culture continues to circulate powerfully in academia and among the public at large, with the advent of new media they no longer serve the purpose they once did. In today's participatory culture, these terms have lost their meaning because the processes they name have become so fluid. The dynamic changes wrought by the digital world call out for a new vocabulary, one as flexible as the history out of which it was born. Just as recent developments have transformed Robert Darnton's radical revision of the publishing circuit (fig. 1), so the academic study of the book needs a vocabulary as vital as its subject.

In *Thinking Outside the Book*, I develop an alternate typology for these key concepts that better fits the needs of today—and also, not inconsequentially, of the past. In searching for a set of terms vibrant enough to repurpose the study of the book for the broadest possible range of functions, I recommend replacing the terms literacy, authorship, publication, edition, and editor with a more self-consciously metaphorical set of keywords. Just as the idea of the book has expanded beyond its material form, so too should our vocabulary reflect how the field of textual production has broadened to include radio, cinema, television, and, perhaps most dramatically in its impact, the Internet.[10] I therefore propose (re)mediation, memory, history, testimony, and loss as terms that better describe the energies now shared across media that we have previously associated with book culture. As the case studies that make up this book will show, these terms also more accurately reflect the "decentralized emergent order" that characterizes complex systems like print culture and other forms of media.[11]

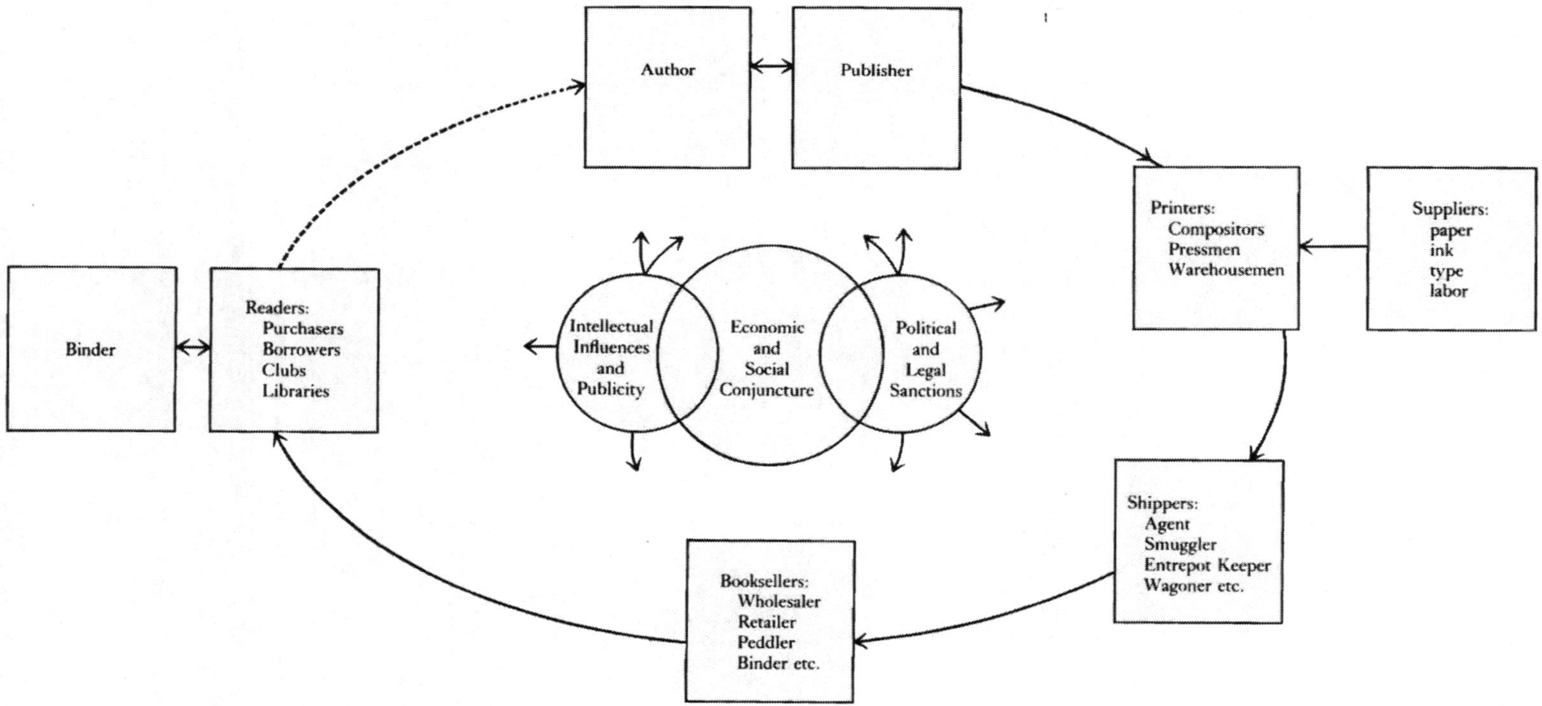

Figure 1. Robert Darnton's map of the publication circuit. From Robert Darnton, "What Is the History of Books?," *Daedalus* 111.3 (1982).

In proposing this new terminology, I emphasize time over space and process over product. Following Carla Hesse, I "reconceptualize the key institutions of modern literary culture . . . in terms of time, motion, and modes of action, rather than in terms of space, objects, and actors."[12] I do so by suggesting that we think of literacy as a form of mediation, authorship as keyed to memory, publication as a foundation for conventional history, the edition as a form of testimony, and the editor as a negotiator of loss. By positing these terms as a series, I do not simply present them as parallel to the traditional terms. Rather, mediation, memory, history, testimony, and loss are meant to operate as what Elizabeth Grosz has termed "active vectors": they are transformative, adjusting the lens to foreground the book as work and rethink the protocols that animate cultural communication.[13]

The MacArthur report reminds us that "the tools available to a culture matter, but what that culture does with those tools matters more."[14] The nineteenth-century women writers at the center of *Thinking Outside the Book* demonstrate that the utility of "the book" is precisely its flexibility, that is, what it can do rather than what it is. Women writers, as a historical group, are bound by several important if conflicting forces. Writings by nineteenth-century women seemed to prevail, at least statistically, in the literary marketplace of their time. These writers were much maligned and constricted, however, by reigning literary tastes mediated through and negotiated by a male-dominated publishing business. The concerns over popular taste, the market, and aesthetic value that characterized nineteenth-century debates about their work remain potent today, as we struggle to define and redefine American literature and culture amidst the shards and fractures that the rise of women's literature foresaw. But my study of nineteenth-century women's writing does not simply reveal the networked quality of the marketplace itself.[15] Rather, I consider, from the limits of historical/literary analysis, the prevalence of the unlikely, the unexpected, and the unaccountable as necessary if neglected factors in making literature. Just as Anthony Grafton's study of the footnote and Patricia Meyer Spacks's work on gossip have yielded deeper understanding of the center from the margins of literary culture, so *Thinking Outside the Book* uses women's writing, a peripheral field that has become central, to explore the limits of literary history and its terminologies.[16] At the same time, the recent rise to dominance of women's writing as a field of study qualifies it as an effective metonym for the professional discourse used to study literature and theorize culture.[17]

In the chapters that follow, I assemble a cohort of literary figures—Jane Johnston Schoolcraft, Sojourner Truth, Hannah Crafts, Augusta Evans, and Mary Chesnut—who challenge the traditional vocabulary of book history. Collectively, their work constitutes an alternative to more familiar women writers, like Harriet Beecher Stowe, referred to by Hawthorne in his famous screed against the "d——d mob of scribbling women," and thus routinely discussed in literary histories. These figures—though unusual—are nonetheless representative of the various strategies authors, editors, and publishers developed in order to capture public interest and cultivate a sense of history-in-the-making. Put into the context of more traditional narratives of the past, a study of their efforts describes a fuller history—one just as important in discussing Dickinson, Emerson, Hawthorne, James, Longfellow, or Thoreau. Like those writers, the cohort under consideration here experimented with literature and literary tastes to the point of innovation. But the fact that this group is not as well known allows me to highlight the epistemological challenges that more traditional figures—writing from the center of the literary canon and subsequent scholarly treatment—might occlude. Thus, though Emerson, for instance, experimented with multiple literacies in his published essays and poems, a focus on how those efforts expand our concept of literacy to the point where we would understand his moves as a form of negotiation would lack the social and cultural urgency bestowed on Jane Johnston Schoolcraft's position as a mixed-race Native American. So too would a focus on Longfellow—whose innovative use of formats and editions expanded the market and cultural relevance of his work as Evans's use of editions has—be overshadowed by attention to his canonical status and the debates over his political and aesthetic values. The writers I focus on have the power to illuminate the larger archive out of which they are drawn partly because the social and cultural factors of race, gender, and region created the space for their challenges and innovations. Just as important, their rise in popularity among academics cannot be explained (away) as historical accuracy enhanced through a focus on the economics of the literary marketplace in which women writers were a dominant force. Rather, these cases reflect the history of cultural adjustments as such and therefore have the power to expose key fissures in our understanding of (literary) culture. Print exposes and obscures the mitigating forces of recovery, creating one archive while also replacing another. *Thinking Outside the Book* overturns the primacy of print as the sine qua non of literary history to probe the question: What is literary in literary history?

These case histories will show how the alternative terminology I present here opens the contours of book history to a broader notion of text. Recent scholarship has struggled to make sense of the massive changes wrought by contemporary economic and technological forces on the literary sphere. From online learning to digital publication, the world of higher education is rapidly moving away from the models that have defined it more or less since the rise of the university in the Middle Ages. New work that addresses these changes typically emphasizes the similarities (or differences) between old and new forms of literature and culture, leaving readers to decide for themselves how much to invest in theories of the new at the expense of the old. *Thinking Outside the Book* is as urgently concerned with the plight of literary studies in the twenty-first century as it is with the literature of the nineteenth century. It thus aligns with the work of scholars, such as Andrew Piper and Kathleen Fitzpatrick, who seek to understand recent changes as synergistic expansions of earlier forms of literary culture and the scholarship they inspired.[18]

Though I undertake several complexly interweaving projects, all of them stem from a belief that the multimodal and continuous process that creates the constitutive roles played by both literary historians and readers is not just a twenty-first-century phenomenon. By revisiting past scenes of literary production, reception, and history, I imagine the story behind, beyond, and between the facts we believe we know. Imbued with a healthy skepticism toward materialist efforts to uncover the past through myriad arcane details, this volume works from the material details of publication to the form and content of literary texts, their producers, and their readers. In order to truly think outside the book and into the twenty-first century, we must focus on the underlying theories of literary culture, and not on its properties.

Earlier studies of the book and literary culture have placed a staggering amount of emphasis on published texts.[19] In *Thinking Outside the Book*, I eschew this publication-centered focus on the single-authored book. Chapter 1, (Re)mediation (Literacy Rethought)," focuses on Jane Johnston Schoolcraft, a mixed-blood Ojibwe woman who was married to the ethnologist John Schoolcraft. Because Schoolcraft's literary life began in the world of oral texts, she mediates the boundary between her native oral Ojibwe culture and contemporary literary/literate life. Her career as scribe and author provides an alternative introduction to nineteenth-century American women's writing that is quite different from the dominant narrative of the white women writers who wrote for the marketplace, including Harriet Beecher Stowe, Susan Warner, and Sara Payson Willis (a.k.a. "Fanny Fern"). Playing on the differences between insider and outsider, Schoolcraft intelligently works her way into a canonized discourse without giving her own tradition short shrift. As perception of Schoolcraft has gone from unknown "scribe" of native Ojibwe oral culture to self-identified poet and published "author," her history emphasizes the range of available literacies and their value as acts of mediation that form cultural memory.

Chapter 2, "Memory (Authorship Revisited)," uses the case of Sojourner Truth to reconsider the relationship between authorship and cultural memory. I argue that Truth, who made a living selling her narrative despite remaining illiterate all her life, saw authorship as a way to consolidate her image and convert it into an icon. Building on the work of Frances Smith Foster, Nell Painter, and Lori Merish, I examine how Truth cannily adapts her text and image to the protocols of authorship in order to forge herself into civic memory. Truth's 1850 *Narrative* (written by Olive Gilbert) went through numerous editions and provided her with an income throughout her life. Her success as an illiterate woman author challenges the norms of print culture, especially in the way she resisted racialized expectations about genre and voice that pushed her toward both literacy and the conventions of the slave narrative. Indeed, Truth's choice to eschew traditional literacy shows how authorship can function in the service of memory even more powerfully than the book.

Chapter 3, "History (Publication Redefined)," works toward a theory of literature, reading, and publication that emphasizes the gap between the codex and the born-digital by examining *The Bondwoman's Narrative* by Hannah Crafts, a semiautobiographical tale written by an African American slave woman.[20] *The Bondwoman's Narrative* is a fugitive text in multiple ways: it tells the story of its author's escape from slavery, and it was not published until 2002, after Henry Louis Gates Jr. discovered and authenticated the manuscript. The intertwined identity of text and author offers us an opportunity to reconsider the meaning of publication and its role in constructing literary history. As both a nineteenth-century unpublished manuscript and a twenty-first-century literary sensation, Crafts's book reflects the function race plays in shaping American literary history, both then and now. According to nineteenth-century standards, *The Bondwoman's Narrative* had to remain a manuscript to succeed in its aesthetic project. In the twenty-first century, that aesthetic project has given way to history as the novel takes its place among a pantheon of "firsts." The 150 years between the writing and publication of the book resolved the fluctuating relationship between editor, publisher, and author, openly recasting authorship as a shared—and historical—position.

Even when my inquiry turns to a traditionally published book, as in chapter 4, "Testimony (The Edition Reimagined)," where I focus on the work of Augusta Jane Evans, the book appears as a collective text, constituted by the multiple nodes of the publishing circuit first described by Robert Darnton and fruitfully developed by Jerome McGann.[21] In chapter 4 the discussion moves back across the color line to investigate the way editions constitute the larger protocols of cultural communication. Traditional scholarship has valued—and even insisted upon—the first edition as its primal scene of interpretation. Here I treat the edition instead as a form of testimony, which detracts from the primacy of the first edition. The study of multiple editions has gained a certain legitimacy in scholarship, in part because of the influence of Marxist and materialist analyses of the book, but that legitimacy pertains only to particular economies. Evans offers us a different way to use multiple editions as a tool for literary history—one that more closely resembles Longfellow's use of editions in multiple formats to reach a broader readership.[22] Her success as an author overcame the ideological differences between North and South: she drew readers from diverse geographic, political, economic, and social backgrounds at a time when those distinctions were fraught with tension. Reviewers in both William Lloyd Garrison's *Liberator* and *The Southern Literary Messenger* discussed *Macaria* (1864). The novel was supposedly smuggled into the North for publication, then banned and burned by Union commanders. As the scholar Melissa Homestead discovered, however, the account of the novel as contraband is actually a foundational myth. In chapter 4 I suggest that this invented origin story, which facilitated *Macaria*'s popularity even after the Civil War, was a functional response intended to excuse Northern enjoyment of the novel. *Macaria* was reprinted six times between 1864 and 1903 and enjoyed brisk sales on both sides of the Mason-Dixon line. Each edition, as I show, documents the developing relationship between North and South before, during, and after the Civil War.

Thinking Outside the Book neither valorizes the unpublished through the lens of the avant-garde nor privileges the symbolic value and material status of the book; rather, it interrogates the relationship between manuscript and published text.[23] To that end, the final chapter focuses on editorial interventions in the three published editions of Mary Boykin Chesnut's so-called diary. "Loss (Authorship Regained)" moves the discussion of editions into the realm of multiple editors. Urged to publish her Civil War writings by Varina Davis, Jefferson Davis's wife, Chesnut revised her text but never published it. Davis predicted that the diary would rival the success of the popular Southern plantation novelists, and she was right. Since its initial publication in 1905, there have been three important editions of the diary, including the "restored" Pulitzer Prize–winning volume prepared by the historian C. Vann Woodward. In rendering Chesnut's efforts to enhance the text's literary value practically null, does this historically minded edition violate principles of authorship? A comparative study of these editions illuminates how Chesnut's editors become writers themselves, as they variously preserve Chesnut's status as "author."

My fundamental goal in this book is to identify a shared purpose between print culture and new media and find a way to elaborate their commonalities without stifling either one. This goal emerged in part in response to the overarching crisis of interpretation and purpose that has surfaced in debates about the value of the past and the function of the humanities in the twenty-first century.[24] In asking what it means to study print culture in a digital age, *Thinking Outside the Book* brings seemingly parallel universes into contact, without unduly consolidating them.

Convergence is this project's guiding principle.[25] From ancient papyrus to the postmodern e-book, the cultural traditions, ritual practices, and rites of passage signified by the book have both endured and been transformed, sometimes beyond recognition. Today we ask: Is the book the Ozymandias of our time, preserved only in its ruins and by our ruminations on its fall?[26] Do our libraries, archives, and universities represent our greatest folly: the belief that we as a species will inevitably endure? Or are our books and libraries our greatest gestures of faith? Informing these questions are even larger issues: the belief that there are such things as coherence and continuity, that they can be represented by the sheer amassing of texts, that survival is linked to remembering, that the archive is about remembering rather than forgetting. These may seem inordinately grand concerns for an academic book. Yet they are precisely the questions and issues that face the humanities as we proceed into the twenty-first century.[27]

Thinking Outside the Book takes up these questions and issues from the vantage point of nineteenth-century America, a period that saw the dramatic rise of print, from the penny press to the best-seller and the serial. Closely examining several key women writers of the time, I link textual production and textual theory to studies of authorship, exploring the various ways in which the collaborations, resistances, and challenges to authorial practices of my focal figures radicalize our thinking about the book itself, the fundamental object of nineteenth-century literary history. The unusual and complex positions of these women within the nineteenth-century literary marketplace challenged the prevailing models of authorship—and help us think about our own radically transforming notions of authors, books, and media. Their "thinking outside the book" can successfully prompt our own.

CHAPTER 1

(Re)Mediation (Literacy Rethought)

In 2007, thanks to an NEH grant, the Ojibwe people finally found a way to preserve their past without transforming it according to the protocols of print.[1] Gibagadinamaagoom, a digital archive developed by Timothy B. Powell and Larry P. Aitken, makes use of "new media's potential to integrate cultural codes and digital codes" in order to "expand the scope of American literature beyond 'the book.'"[2]

The Web format is especially congenial to a tribal culture that expresses its history in a medium other than print. As Powell and Aitken explain, "digital technology is valuable because its interactive qualities allow viewers to ask the elders about their history, to look into their eyes, and to hear chi-ayy ya agg speak in their own language and on their own cultural terms."[3] Yet the synergy between Ojibwe epistemic practices and a multimodal digital environment entails more than mere alignment. The Ojibwe model of cultural production anticipated the interactivities facilitated by the Internet in the twenty-first century. Print-based models of literacy, by contrast, not only inhibited the transmission of American Indian cultures but also, in relegating those cultures to what Powell and Aitken call "the margins of the white page,"[4] continue to muffle Native American expression.

Long before the advent of the Internet, Jane Johnston Schoolcraft, a mixed-blood Ojibwe woman married to the Anglo-American ethnologist Henry Rowe Schoolcraft, challenged the limits of print literacy. Her writings enact and commemorate Ojibwe cultural practices, interpolating the sounds of her tribal culture into a linear textual environment.[5] The archive of her work offers a parallactic view of our contemporary struggles to reckon with multimodal digital culture as both product and practice. Her strategies to preserve, extend, and commemorate her sophisticated blend of cultures and literacies provide important lessons on how we might grapple with our own complicated tangle of communication protocols.

At the same time, Schoolcraft's work traces an alternative trajectory for the woman writer, one that significantly differs from the dominant narrative of white women who wrote for the nineteenth-century marketplace, such as Harriet Beecher Stowe, Susan Warner, and Sara Payson Willis (a.k.a. "Fanny Fern"). She thus invites us to consider not just what is "oral" about "oral literature" but also what is "literary" about "literature" itself. In this chapter I parse Schoolcraft's archive into four categories—the reprinted tale, the pseudonymous poem, the poem that appeared under her own full name, and the untranslated poem—in order to explore the complexities of her negotiations between two competing and often incommensurate literacies. In the end, the space Schoolcraft stakes out between "scribe" and "author," "speech" and "writing," the book as work and as text provides a useful model for twenty-first-century literacies.[6]

Jane Johnston Schoolcraft and the Culture of the Book

Jane Johnston Schoolcraft was raised in a mixed-race household, the daughter of an Ojibwe mother and an Irish immigrant father. Her mother, Ozhaguscodaywayquay, later known as Susan, was the daughter of Waubojeeg, an important Ojibwe war chief, and had an illustrious tribal past. She spoke to her children only in Ojibwe and taught them the Ojibwe traditions. Schoolcraft's father, John Johnston, passed his love of literature down to his daughter by encouraging her and the rest of the household to write poetry, as he did, and by allowing her free access to his large personal library. This complexly layered past resonates throughout Schoolcraft's archive, which preserves a set of discrete decoding skills that model the value of multiple and overlapping literacies.[7]

Schoolcraft was the first American Indian woman to "publish" in the United States. These scare quotes are purposeful, for although Schoolcraft's descriptions of Ojibwe practices, Ojibwe tales (transcribed and translated), and original poetry appeared in various forms of print, they did not necessarily do so in ways that allowed her recognition as their author. Some of her writing was subsumed into her husband's ethnological studies; other pieces were handwritten by her husband and other family members in a homemade literary "magazine" and attributed to a pen name (she had several). Her work thus reveals how dramatically print conventions can shape perceptions of cultural legitimacy. Granting Schoolcraft the status of author bestows upon her—and other Native peoples—the cultural legitimacy that comes with having a literary history.[8] In granting this status, I replace hoary conflicts about literacy and the nature of authorship with a purposeful act of (re)mediation, foregrounding efforts to repair or remedy the historical damage done to Native peoples.

Although *The Literary Voyager; or, Muzzenyegun* (1826–27) circulated in Detroit, New York, and Schoolcraft's native Sault Ste. Marie, its status as a magazine was largely rhetorical. The publication was more than a scrapbook, because it circulated through handwritten copies, numbered like a serial publication; but that circulation more properly replicates the gift economy as described by Leon Jackson than any nineteenth-century publishing model.[9] In this case, as it passed among interested parties, *The Literary Voyager* made its profits in social interest and engagement.[10] Henry Schoolcraft created *The Literary Voyager* to promote and provide evidence for his work as the first federal Indian agent and ethnographer. As he staked out his professional ground, he guided his "voyage" more than metaphorically, selecting and arranging all of the magazine's material while leaving much of the transcribing to his wife.

The magazine's name indicates its cultural purpose from the very beginning. The first phrase reflects its proposed English-speaking readership and affirms those readers' position of power. Placing the English rendering before the Ojibwe, the title reverses the principle of translation that Roger Williams radically enacted when he placed the Algonkian words before their English translations in *A Key into the Language of America* (1643). Interestingly, the secondary title, though preceded by "or," is neither a translation nor, as it may appear, a cognate; rather, *muzzenyegun* is the Ojibwe word for book. According to Louise Erdrich, the root *mazina* turns up in "dozens of words, all concerned with made images and with the substances upon which

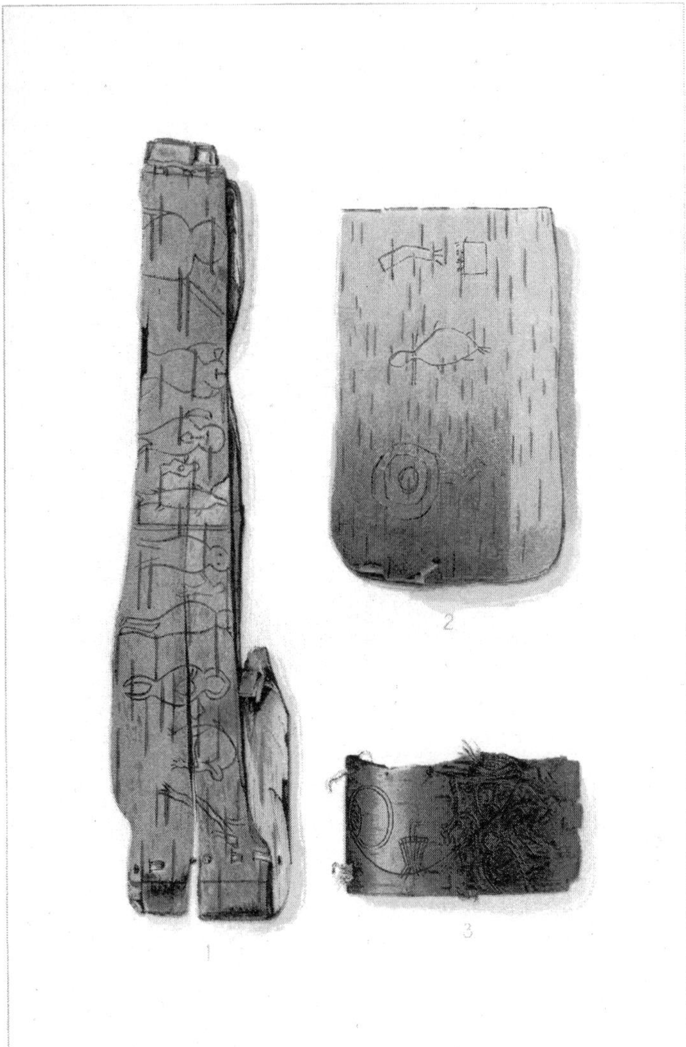

Figure 2. Scrolls of the Mide'wiwin, or "Grand Medicine Society," of the Ojibwe, from the "Seventh Annual Report of the Bureau of Ethnology to the Secretary of the Smithsonian Institution," 1885–1866. Courtesy of Washington State University, Holland-Terrill Library, Manuscripts, Archives, and Special Collections.

images are put, mainly paper or screens."[11] An earlier iteration of *muzzenyegun* is *mazinibaganjigan*, the Ojibwe name for the first books made in North America.[12] *Mazinibaganjigan* are dental pictographs made by bite marks on birch bark, known to have been in existence for thousands of years, predating any Anglo book (fig. 2).

Rather than being inscribed or imported, then, the Ojibwe word asserts the culture's claim to the book on its own terms and in its own time. In other words, the second element of the magazine's title pushes back against the first, promoting the Ojibwe creator over the Anglo reader. The full title ultimately signals the tension between the Ojibwe as product of the literary voyage and producer of the *muzzenyegun*. Indeed, most scholars have come to accept the notion that, as Arnold Krupat puts it, "Native American conceptions of history and modern Western conceptions of history are not merely perspectivally different—a matter of vantage point—but epistemologically different, a matter of different ways of perceiving, understanding, and representing the world in narrative."[13] No degree of recognition, however, can undo the racial and colonialist politics of Native-European cultural contact. Even if both poststructuralism and American Indian conceptions of time, space, and history allot a certain primacy to the historical presence and inscription of *muzzenyegun*, we cannot forget that the word—and the magazine—inhabit an Anglo-American world that values originality and position over community and tradition.[14]

Legacy through Literacy: The Reprinted Tale

Until the 2009 appearance of Robert Dale Parker's edited volume *The Sound the Stars Make Rushing through the Sky: The Writings of Jane Johnston Schoolcraft*, Schoolcraft 's legacy rested on her work as a translator of tribal tales rather than on her productions as a single author.[15] Typically identified in their titles by the tagline as "A Chippewa Tale," these stories provide readers outside the community with expressions of a primitive culture that has been eclipsed.[16] This narrative framework situates the story in a marginalized—if not extinct—position with neither cultural status nor power.

One such story, "The Forsaken Brother," has enjoyed a long literary life, surviving in several iterations. First published in the February 13, 1827, issue of *The Literary Voyager*, it was reprinted in four of Henry Schoolcraft's ethnographic studies of American Indians between 1839 and 1856. Robert Dale Parker's meticulous tracking has revealed that the tale also exists in several states in manuscript. Contemporary readers can find it in *The Heath Anthology of American Literature*.[17]

"The Forsaken Brother" tells the story of an Indian family living alone in a remote spot. The tale likens the desolation of its setting to "the long sleep of death" that is about to engulf the family's patriarch, who, in his dying words, commands his eldest son and daughter always to remain with their younger brother so they can protect and nurture him. The older siblings promise to obey their father's wishes, and he dies happy in the knowledge that his children will remain together. Soon enough, however, the older brother and sister become restless and leave the solitude of the family's lodge to join larger village communities. Eventually (and predictably), the youngest son is left alone to fend for himself. He finds comfort and support from a pack of wolves. Adopted, as it were, into their family, he roams the shores of the lake, where one day the older brother thinks he hears the cry of his younger brother. The closer the older brother gets, the more wolf-like the young boy becomes, as he sings about turning into a wolf. Eventually he thoroughly metamorphoses, and the older brother and sister are left to regret their broken promise for the rest of their lives.

Both contemporaneous and current readers have taken "The Forsaken Brother" as a primitive origin tale (or myth) of the sometimes shockingly childlike sound made by a howling wolf. But this interpretation seems conditioned by the generic conventions of print culture that label the story "A Chippewa Tale." The tale's ongoing popularity suggests that it has continued to serve a cultural purpose, but it is rarely clear what—or whose—that purpose is. It is certain, however, that although the political function of the tale may have changed as it moved from performance to print, print retains a degree of stability that orality lacks.

There are several important differences between oral and written tales.[18] There is, of course, the ever-fluctuating (and thus radically unstable) role of gestural, tonal, and verbal variation that shapes each telling of an oral tale; but the aspect of performance on which I want to focus is occasion.[19] Occasion forms a significant context for the tale as performed, suggesting how its meaning will be unpacked. Considered in the context of a culture besieged by encroaching colonial forces—French, British, and finally American—the tale seems to promote solidarity and cultural preservation through family ties. After all, as the sister points out to the departing older brother: "We were not prohibited the society of our fellow mortals, but we were told to cherish each other, and that we should do nothing independent of each other—that neither pleasure nor pain ought ever to separate us, particularly from our helpless brother. If we follow our separate gratifications, it will surely make us forget *him* whom we are alike bound to support" (*Writings*, 178). That is, the idea is not to shun others but to remain together. As divergent as the origin myth and family preservation readings might seem, the differences in interpretation can be tracked through the value placed on literacy, the principle of authorship, and the meaning of originality in determining authorship.

The mere fact that the tale has been translated emphasizes the importance of literacy and asserts the tale's value as a mediating object. Offered to readers (rather than listeners) as a relic of a bygone culture, the "Chippewa Tale" is stabilized and preserved by print. Yet print also serves to nullify the oral tale's aesthetic value; instead, Schoolcraft's artistry ascends as she translates and transcribes the tale, inserting it into a different frame of cultural reference. Schoolcraft casts herself in the role of the participant observer whose literacy and artistry transform the fluid oral text into a stable—and ever available—literary text (much like the local color fiction that would be popular by the end of the century). And though we don't know if Schoolcraft read the Grimm brothers or Aesop, her readers certainly view her Ojibwe stories through their lens.[20] Indeed, without the stabilizing pattern of the folktale, the Ojibwe story might have a completely different meaning to the literate reader.

We can see how thoughtfully Schoolcraft mediates between her two cultures, honoring the primacy of oral culture by emphasizing the aural, rather than the visual, in the published tale.[21] Pivotal moments in the story are oral, foregrounding the value of the Ojibwe tradition. The dying patriarch's children make their initial promise in speech. Perhaps even more important, the older brother initially recognizes his younger brother through sound: "It happened his brother was fishing in his canoe in the lake, a considerable distance out, when he thought he heard the cry of a child, and wondered how any could exist on so bleak a part of the shore. He listened again more attentively, and distinctly heard the cry repeated" (*Writings*, 179). Orality is foregrounded again when the older brother recognizes his sibling, who is "singing in a plaintive voice" (*Writings*, 179).

But Anglo readers would not recognize his song. By transliterating the Ojibwe verse, rather than translating or even simply describing it, Schoolcraft emphasizes the tale's Indian origins. After fluently reading the story's simple diction, an English speaker will stumble on the unfamiliar assemblage of vowels and consonants: "Neesya, neeysa, shyegwuh gushuh! / Ween ne myeengunish! / Ne myeengunish!" (My brother, my brother, / I am now turning into a Wolf!— / I am turning into a wolf")

(*Writings*, 179).[22] The absence of italics, the conventional typographical marker for another language, suggests that though the Ojibwe words may be unfamiliar to the Anglo-American reader, they are not alien. Any reader, for instance, can notice the familiar use of repetition. Inserting the poetic device known as the refrain, Schoolcraft both preserves the story's original cultural formation and remediates Anglo-American literary culture.[23] Here, as elsewhere, Schoolcraft gives us a "double exposure," helping us see how Native and Anglo-American practices might come together without being homogenized. Actively engaging the norms from both cultures, she creates a dynamic circuit of exchange in which Ojibwe words signal the tribal presence whose extinction the English tale narrates.

Marginal Claims: Pseudonymous Poetry

In addition to Ojibwe tales, Schoolcraft contributed original poetry to *The Literary Voyager*, although she mainly published it under the pen names "Rosa" and "Leelinau." The pen name links Schoolcraft's poems, including "By an *Ojibwa Female* Pen," the focus of this section, to the poetess tradition: it obscures (or "dissolves," as Eliza Richards would say) the specificity of her identity—as wife of the ethnographer and editor of the magazine—while accentuating her status as a primitive Other.[24] "By an *Ojibwa Female* Pen" is significant for its connections, spelled out in its title, to cultural assumptions about American Indian identity, gender, and literacy. Like her tales, Schoolcraft's poems written in English register the tension between two worlds: she may use the standard metrical patterns of Anglo-American verse, but vestiges of her struggle to negotiate this tension in her poetry remain.

An earlier manuscript version of "By an *Ojibwa Female* Pen" suggests that the poem was originally titled "Invitation to a walk in the Garden, after a light Shower of rain." The new title, with "Ojibwa" and "Female" italicized, suggests that Henry Schoolcraft may have intervened editorially to emphasize the poem's status as an ethnographical "specimen."[25] Yet Schoolcraft (presumably) retained her initial title in a secondary position as the poem's subtitle: there is a blank line between "By an *Ojibwa Female* Pen" and the italicized "*Invitation to sisters to a walk in the Garden, after a shower.*"[26] As with the title of the magazine, this secondary title underscores the power struggle between Jane Johnston Schoolcraft as author and as American Indian specimen. Nonetheless, the poem's subtitle still performs several important tasks, preserving a degree of agency against the title's ethnographic objectivizing and declaring the voluntary mood and mode of the poem *as an invitation.*

By an *Ojibwa Female* Pen

Invitation to sisters to a walk in the Garden, after a shower

Come, sisters come! The shower's past,
The garden walks are drying fast,
The Sun's bright beams are seen again,
And naught within, can now detain.
The rain drops tremble on the leaves,
Or drip expiring, from the eaves;
But soon the cool and balmy air,
Shall dry the gems that sparkle there,
With whisp'ring breath shake ev'ry spray,
And scatter every cloud away.

Thus sisters! shall the breeze of hope,
Though sorrow's clouds a vista ope;
Thus, shall affliction's surly blast,
By faith's bright calm be still'd at last;
Thus pain and care,—the tear and sigh,
Be chased from every dewy eye;
And life's mix'd scene itself, but cease,
To show us realms of light and peace.

(*Writings*, 108)

The speaker and the sisters are familiar with both American Indian beliefs in the natural world and the poetic practices of Western culture. Framed as an "invitation," the poem identifies and enjoins its readers with the simultaneously imperative and exclamatory "Come, sisters come!" This opening emphasizes its urgency in the quickness of its tetrameter and the sibilant "s" sounds that continue throughout the poem's initial lines. Schoolcraft thus demonstrates her authority through the poem's fluent use of the key protocols of poetry, including rhyme and meter.

The poem's orderly couplets move the reader along, mirroring the sense of optimism and confidence that the passing storm leaves in its wake. No muddy puddles or sloppy paths await these walkers; rather, the remaining raindrops are "gems that sparkle," while the air (not even wind) will "scatter every cloud away." The stanza ends with the vista of a clear, beautiful day, and the open vowel rhymes of the closing couplet ("spray . . . away") underscore the sense of optimism. Sure-footed and clear-eyed, the speaker demonstrates her strength throughout, issuing an invitation, speaking in the imperative, and reassuring her readers that it is the right time for a walk. Yet she nonetheless remains a mystery: formal rhyming couplets may create a space for her to speak, but we do not know who she is or who her sisters are.

The second stanza shifts away from a literal landscape. As signaled by the formal rhetoric of "Thus," the speaker now seems to be addressing a constituency of readers whose consciousness is shaped by Western traditions. Whereas the first stanza uses literal references to suggest a strong belief in the meaningfulness of nature, the second stanza relies on metaphor, a rhetorical form, to make meaning. Both as a formal strategy and as a poetic device, metaphor specifies an agreed-upon set of values and thus identifies its users, in this case both writer and reader, as part of the rhetorical community. In the first stanza all, including language, is clear in the light of day, but the second stanza requires a level of processing—and explication—that the speaker did not need to communicate with her audience in the first. Vindicating the power of nature's message for those who are not familiar with nature's ways, the speaker uses metaphor to broadly translate her own message.

But translation comes at a cost—the loss of meaning—that Schoolcraft signals through compression. The first stanza has ten lines, but the second has just eight, creating an imbalance. Rather than replicating the number of lines and the rhyme scheme of the first stanza, the second reinscribes its meaning in terms that an Anglo-American reader will understand according to generic norms associated with poetry as a written and published form. Invoking "the breeze of hope," "sorrow's clouds," and other conventional Anglo-American poetic tropes, Schoolcraft presents nature as a mediator between two worlds. For the reader of the second stanza, a "breeze" is no longer intrinsically meaningful but must be anthropomorphized through poetry. Yet although metaphor can compress and mediate, it fails to improve upon the first stanza.

The poem's stable rhyme scheme associates it with Anglicized forms of metric poetry popular in the nineteenth century and connects it, not surprisingly, with "Poetess poetics."[27] Yet the orderly couplets and the spareness of the tetrameter also accentuate the ways in which the poem cooperates with—and even capitalizes upon—the association of Native American culture with simplicity. Like much of Schoolcraft's work, the poem bears witness to her relationship and complicity with nineteenth-century poetics, especially as highlighted in the first stanza by the sight rhyme of the second couplet. The poem aligns itself with Romanticism by drawing on the natural formations of family ("Come, sisters") and weather ("The shower's past"), while also emphasizing its strict adherence to the formal demands of meter by repeatedly eliding syllables ("whisp'ring," "ev'ry," "still'd," "mix'd").

Schoolcraft's use of form once again serves a dual purpose. Whereas in her native Ojibwe she relies heavily on repetition as a unifying device, in English she depends on a stable rhyme pattern. Yet even as her rhymes reflect Anglicized forms, they also retain a semblance of orality: though the poem's elisions accommodate its rhyme scheme, they also mirror the spoken word.[28] In other words, she manages to reserve her radical indigeneity through the remedial work of Anglicized poetic forms: conventional rhyme patterns function as a cover for her commitment to Ojibwe oral culture.[29] Her bilinguality is thus also a kind of biliteracy. Though the location of the "realms of light and peace" is not at all clear, the oppositional "but" argues against a reading focused purely on a rather evangelical notion of the afterlife, and instead keeps the reader's attention on the world at hand: "the gems that sparkle there."

If the published version of "The Forsaken Brother" makes a space for Ojibwe language, culture, and orality, Schoolcraft's poetry keeps alive what Bethany Schneider calls "the dynamism of the 'middle ground's' métis culture" by "mixing" literacies.[30] As Robert Dale Parker remarks, "Schoolcraft's writing lays out a model of aesthetic and cultural rather than identitarian representation for Indian writing, while nevertheless carrying forth identitarian representation in its engagement with Indian language and literacy."[31] Both "The Forsaken Brother" and "By an *Ojibwa Female* Pen" affirm writing as a powerful tool for negotiating difference without simply recapitulating the traditions of dominant Anglo-American culture.

Provisional Authorship

Schoolcraft did publish poetry under her own name in *The Literary Voyager.* The elegy "To my ever beloved & lamented Son William Henry," which appeared under her full name, exists in at least seven versions, exceeding any other poem she wrote in number of both copies and versions.[32] This multiplicity indicates both the artistic effort she put into the poem and its value to her.

After their toddler son died on February 13, 1827, the Schoolcrafts filled an issue of *The Literary Voyager* with memorials written by family and friends.[33] A moving collection of prose and verse, the issue was "published" a little over a month after their son's passing. It begins with a simple death notice: "Died, / On the 13th inst. At 11 o'clock at night, William Henry, only child of Henry R. Schoolcraft Esqr. Æ. 2 years, 8 mo. & 14 days. 'Suffer little children to come unto me, and forbid them not; for of such is the kingdom of heaven'" (*Literary Voyager*, 144). Modeled after a newspaper death notice, the announcement is followed by a solid line across the page, reminiscent of black-bordered mourning stationery. Indeed, we might see this line as a visual representation of the divide between Ojibwe and Anglo-American mourning practices, but like the texts that follow, it fails to preserve the boundaries it appears to demarcate.

The next text is a brief narrative of the child's life, which situates his origins in the season and land of his birth: "The month of May [1824] at the Sault Ste. Marie, was a month of all the sweets of attractive northern climate and scenery. The harsh winds of winter, had ceased with the opening of April. May introduced into the woodlands and glades of the St. Mary's valley, the little pink bordered *miscodeed*, or spring beauty, the wild violet of the north" (*Literary Voyager*, 144). These lines sensualize the landscape, blurring the boundaries between the senses with weather and landscape one can taste: "all the sweets of attractive northern climate and scenery." The "beautiful and bright-eyes, little stranger William Henry" takes his place among "Flora's bounties," yet despite this emphasis on natural order, the child's multiracial status is played down. He is described as having "a face of the purest Caucasian whiteness" before being fitted to a model of American identity that emphasizes multiethnic origins. That the child's "mother was another Pocahontas, Chippewa blood by the maternal line, and a sire from . . . the north of Ireland," increased interest in the "bright American boy, and many visits were paid to see the mother and child" (*Literary Voyager*, 144–45).

William Henry's "mix'd scene" is a central feature of the chronicle of his short life, which stresses both his bilinguality and his biculturality: "His grandmother, never failed to address him in the native tongue, and used both the Chippewa and English words, sometimes as synonyms, and sometimes by clipping the Indian of its initial, or terminal syllables. She invariably addressed him by native infantile expression for boys, penaysee or little Bird, a term of manly endearment, birds being symbolically, referred to as figures of speech in war. And she carefully made him a little pillow of swan's down, plucked from the game brought in by aboriginal friends" (*Literary Voyager*, 146). The developing narrative invites the reader to see a harmonious relationship between the two traditions. Just as the Indian word "penaysee" is not italicized, so it is assumed that the reader is amenable to cultural mixing and code switching. William Henry's principal playthings, wooden alphabet blocks made by his father and a small cache of cornelians and agates from Lake Huron, represent his two heritages functioning comfortably together, nurturing the child's sense of pleasure and developing intellect. The combination of the alphabet and the stones returns at the end of his story: "In the spring a neat tombstone of marble was erected, containing under the dates, the words 'Sweet Willy.' His vase of agates were spread around the path, and the mountain ash, and the rose and wild violets planted, as a shade, over the sacred spot" (*Literary Voyager*, 147–48). The emphasis on the story's temporal symmetry, beginning and ending with spring, reflects the effort to normalize this inexplicable loss as part of the cycle of life. What is notable throughout the memorial is the effort to find a pattern—and thus some sensible reason—to compensate for the loss of this beloved child.

Despite the plethora of intimate detail, the author of the prose memorial is never identified, lending the account a degree of objectivity. In contrast, the following poem foregrounds its author's identity in its very title: "Lines of a Father on the Death of His Son." The poem has three asymmetrical stanzas and regular rhyming couplets. In the formal tension between them, Henry Schoolcraft represents both the jagged nature of his pain and his unrelenting grief. Framed as social duty rather than artistic expression, the poem begins, "Sad is the task, a father's hand essays, / To mourn thy fate in tributary lays" (*Literary Voyager*, 148). Appended to a letter sent to his wife, Jane, Henry's couplets depicting home life proceed in orderly rhyming couplets. Form cannot and will not provide a respite.

If Henry Schoolcraft deploys poetic form to represent the pain of his loss, his wife both evokes and resists traditional Anglo-American mourning practices in "To my ever beloved & lamented Son William Henry," the one poem in the issue addressed directly to the dead child. "Ever Beloved" is also the only piece in the issue that includes the full name of its author. (Others are identified by initials or pen names, including Schoolcraft's own, "Rosa.") In contrast to the generic tribal affiliation of "By an *Ojibwa Female* Pen," this text uses Schoolcraft's married name. It thus, on the one hand, trades on her status as mother of the dead child to align her suffering with the broader tradition of elegy, and, on the other, distances her from the poetess tradition, thus insisting on her own relation to Anglo-American cultural practices. (Henry Schoolcraft absurdly described the poem as "fit to be preserved as a specimen of native composition.") Refusing to dissolve her identity in a pen name, she asserts a sense of self and place through the byline "Jane Johnson Schoolcraft." Claiming authorship of the poem as her own, she ultimately makes herself its subject while also demanding a place for herself in the Anglo-American tradition of authorship.

Schoolcraft clearly modeled "Ever Beloved" on Margaret Taylor's popular poem "My Mother." She used the same rhyme pattern, quoted Taylor, and adapted the refrain to suit her subject: instead of repeating "My mother" at the close of each stanza, she alternates between "My Willy" and "Sweet Willy."[34] By using Taylor as a reference point, Schoolcraft accentuates her pain as it contrasts to the pleasures Taylor describes. The poem's song-like quality, emphasized by the alternating refrain, links it to oral culture, as does its call-and-response pattern. The first lines of each stanza are answered by the refrain: "Who was it, nestled on my breast, / And on my cheek sweet kisses prest / And in whose smile I felt so blest? / Sweet Willy" (*Literary Voyager*, 150). One critical way in which Schoolcraft deviates from her model, however, is by changing the poem's point of view, establishing an alternative power dynamic. In Taylor's poem, the child addresses the mother, paying homage and pledging ongoing gratitude in lines like "Who fed me from her gentle breast / And hushed me in her arms to rest / And on my cheek sweet kisses prest? / My Mother." Schoolcraft's poem reverses this dynamic. The mother needs the child: "Who was it, wiped my tearful eye, / And kiss'd away the coming sigh, / And smiling bid me say 'good boy' / Sweet Willy" (*Literary Voyager*, 150). Schoolcraft thus both claims Taylor's tradition of motherhood and deviates from it.

Schoolcraft's circumstances reinforce her departure from Taylor's model. The child in her poem dies in the fifth stanza ("But oh! That soul has flown above"), and the rest of the poem contends with the mother's reaction to her loss, a loss unimaginable to the youthful maternal speaker of Taylor's poem. The mother in "Ever Beloved" has been traumatically shorn of the pleasures Taylor's poem promises: enduring gratitude and loyalty. Unable to fold her feelings into the formal practices of Anglo-American mourning through elegy, Schoolcraft ultimately makes her own suffering her subject, and the poem ends up twice as long as Taylor's yet hardly compensates for her loss. Like the failure of the solid line below the death notice to form an impervious boundary between death and those left behind, the formal elegy fails to provide comfort or support for this grieving mother.

After "To my ever beloved & lamented Son William Henry" appeared in *The Literary Voyager*, Henry Schoolcraft sent a copy to C. C. Trowbridge, whose publishing connections in Detroit made him an important contact for Schoolcraft's poetic future. The lines struck him "with such peculiar force as well in regard to the pathos of style as the single felicity of expression" that he took "the liberty to submit them to the Governor who has advised me to publish them."[35] State-sanctioned, the poem seemed poised to reach a wider readership, but when informed of the opportunity, Schoolcraft appears to have declined; certainly it was not published. Though we have no evidence of her reasons for refusing publication, the event offers rich opportunity for speculation. Given Henry Schoolcraft's track record of using his wife's work without attribution, it seems likely that he sent off the poem without her knowledge; but given the poem's personal nature, it seems doubtful that he would have published it without her permission. The fact that he did publish the poem after her death suggests that she was the one who withheld it.

The poem has several features that might have dissuaded her from sharing it with the wide readership of a Detroit newspaper. For one thing, it noticeably lacks any representation, formal or linguistic, of a tie to Ojibwe culture. Indeed, the poem violates a basic principle of Ojibwe mourning by shifting the focus from the deceased to the mother and her loss.[36] Historical Ojibwe mourning practices include destruction of the deceased's personal property and a prolonged break from hunting.[37] In contrast, the poem represents Schoolcraft carrying on with her profession of writing. Her turn to the Euro-American elegy, like her use of Taylor, sways the text's balance from the "middle ground" characteristic of much of her work to a decidedly Anglicized frame of reference. It may very well be that, despite the many versions of the poem that Parker suggests indicate her particular pride in it, Schoolcraft ultimately did not want to be identified in such Anglophilic terms. Rather than capitulate to the dominant culture by publishing her elegy, she chose to leave it to the archive. The archive thus shows us how Schoolcraft registered points of contact between two traditions that ultimately remain unbridgeable.

Staging Difference

The final element of Schoolcraft's archive is the poems she wrote in Ojibwe and did not translate. These poems represent all-out resistance to dominant cultural formations, speaking for themselves as poems meant for a particular readership. One such poem was written after she placed her two surviving children in boarding school. The poem was later translated by her husband and published after her death; yet, as Bethany Schneider shows, Henry Schoolcraft's translation, which he termed "free," bears little resemblance to the original. Not only did he transform the poem into a formal elegy, even though the children were alive, but also the translated poem is considerably longer than the original. To say that Henry Schoolcraft exerts control over the poem through his translation is only to begin to understand the degree of its transformation.

Schoolcraft's archive makes it clear that her decision to keep the poem in Ojibwe has a powerful purpose. By using her mother tongue, Schoolcraft protects the poem's subjects, her children, from outsiders. (Even I cannot directly discuss her Ojibwe poems without the mediation of a translation.) Writing in Ojibwe also protects her poem from alteration by the dominant formations of print, such as the elegy ultimately imposed upon it by Henry Schoolcraft.[38] Schoolcraft retains control over the poem in two other notable ways. She left it untitled, emphasizing its inscrutable status as a poem that could not be incorporated into the larger archive of titled poems in English. She also wrote the poem without punctuation marks, rejecting these crucial signifiers of print and instead emphasizing the relationship to her oral Ojibwe culture.[39]

These Ojibwe poems represent Schoolcraft's most radical efforts to retain control over herself and her children in an aggressively Anglo-American context. These materials could not—and would not—be reprinted in her husband's ethnographies without translation. And when they were translated, the translations, as Schneider shows, reveal the drive for cultural dominance and control that we have come to associate with mid-nineteenth-century ethnography, and with Henry Schoolcraft in particular. Keeping the poems in Ojibwe left a recognizable space in the archive for stretching that archive's very limits, much as its founders hope to do with Gibagadinamaagoom. As tribal elder Larry Aitken observes: "The center of our culture has always been our language. If we lose our language, we lose it all. But there are always those who hang on."[40] These poems are evidence that Schoolcraft hung on.

Remediating Literacy from Scribe to Author: A Critical Round-Up

Schoolcraft's work has allowed us to identify the ability to remediate (repair or correct) relationships between and among people as a primary goal of literacy. Rather than reproducing the well-known rift between American Indian and Anglo-American cultural practices along the oral-print divide, Schoolcraft's sophisticated efforts to engage, transform, and move beyond the limits of genre produce a "mix'd scene." Defining her as either a "scribe" or an "author" limits the epistemological impact her work can have if it is freed from those categories. "Scribe" undervalues her contribution to the texts she produced, while "author" overstresses notions of individuality and originality that are central to traditional definitions of authorship but do not accurately describe her archive. Just as Schoolcraft seems to have put aside the offer to publish her elegy in order to preserve her own sense of social and cultural balance, so must we put aside the rigid typologies that have kept scribes and authors partitioned from the larger flows of multiple literacies.

Schoolcraft's work also provides a model through which we can undertake a critical examination of literacy and of the book as a cultural formation.[41] Her complicated relationships with her Indian culture as a mixed-race woman, compounded by her marriage to an Anglo-American ethnologist, place Schoolcraft in precisely the "literate-performative network" that produces deeply reciprocal outcomes, according to Joshua Bellin: in his terms, "an intercultural performative bundle."[42] For Schoolcraft, whose life straddled two cultures, the working together of Ojibwe and Anglo-American cultural markers would have been an existential necessity as long as she wished to preserve her past and forge a future for herself and her family. As Bellin urges, "rather than rejecting the texts of Indian-white encounter as a derivative or diminishment of a sacred original—or accepting these texts only as a regrettable concession to the futility of rescuing an oral-performative prototype," we should recognize that these texts have a restorative power "as a necessary aspect of the medicine bundle, existing in tension and relation with other aspects within the larger performative network."[43] Schoolcraft's archive does remedial work, stitching together cultures and constituencies.

Literacy, the sine qua non of literary culture, is determined by what Lisa Gitelman identifies as an "economy of records and documents—aesthetic and nonaesthetic."[44] I have focused here on (aesthetic) form and the ways in which literary history's (non-aesthetic) method of record keeping fuses the significantly distinct registers in Schoolcraft's work. Archives, and the reception histories they promote, are constructed according to genre and the expectations genre creates.[45] The available categories—scribe, author, even poet—obscure a richer and more dialogic history. Of the terms we might use to describe Schoolcraft's blend of tradition, community, orality, and print, none leaves sufficient conceptual room for Schoolcraft's straddling of communal oral traditions and the capitalistic preferences of print culture.

Reconceptualizing literacy itself as a form of mediation also provides us with a useful opportunity to rethink a problem we associate with contemporary digital culture. The forms of publication made possible by the Internet are enmeshed in the political and social limits that defined publication in the nineteenth century. The Web depends on a labyrinth of complex systems that guide and shape cultural production, all the while creating a paradoxical mix of freedom and control that registers in every dimension, from production to access. Attending carefully to Schoolcraft's archive helps us remain aware of the multiple registers in which she operated. The layered quality preserved in that archive manifests the practical limits of print while anticipating the philosophical aims of Gibagadinamaagoom. If Schoolcraft could have accessed the multimodal Web technologies available on the Internet, she might have been able to synchronize her archive with her aesthetic and cultural choices in a way that she could never achieve in conventional print formats. Yet, as we peel back the layers we use to maintain multiple forms as discrete, even if overlapping, we find a new and confining limit: the information architecture we use to build Internet archives. From Omeka to Drupal—to name just two open-source content management frameworks used to build Internet archives—users must adapt to existing forms while also seeking to transform them.

Each of the four categories of Schoolcraft's archive offers a fresh opportunity to rethink literacy as a central placeholder of literary history. Unspooling the layers of her diverse output reveals how literacy and literary history have been consolidated. In reviving the critical importance of difference, in terms of both culture and literacy, we need not balkanize the paradigms that difference creates. Rather, we can uncover an alternate typology on which another literary history might be built. Looking at Schoolcraft's bilinguality as biliteracy recalibrates the power dynamics between Native and Anglo-American cultures. Playing on the differences between insider and outsider, Schoolcraft intelligently works her way into a canonized discourse without giving her own tradition short shrift. Recognizing the value of code switching for the bilingual/biliterate writer and reader, we can grasp the importance (and beauty) of Schoolcraft's project. In the spectrum from unknown "scribe" of Native Ojibwe oral culture to self-identified poet and, today, published "author," her history highlights all kinds of literacy as acts of remediation.

Schoolcraft's archive also shows how print both exposes and obscures the mitigating forces of recovery. The history of this archive, including its contemporary recovery, makes manifest the redemptive quality of archiving itself. In aggregating the past, we redraw it according to our own principles, whether they are articulated or not. This redrawing is not only theoretical but also practical, as the digital archive offers its own new principles with burgeoning possibilities of organization and representation on all levels. Rethinking literacy as (re)mediation better positions us to move forward into twenty-first-century theories of the book that are not bound by the codex but grow out of it.

CHAPTER 2

Memory (Authorship Revisited)

If, for many Native American tribes, literacy represented a certain capitulation to white culture, for African Americans it was a first step toward freedom. Not only were slaves denied education, but also in most states, efforts to teach them to read and write were actionable by law. Nevertheless, slaves still found methods to acquire literacy, which helped them in two material ways: it enabled them to write their own passes and, more significantly here, to write autobiographies, whose proceeds could be used to buy themselves and their families out of slavery. From the first successful slave narrative, written by Olaudah Equiano, to the renowned *Narrative of the Life of Frederick Douglass, An American Slave, Written by Himself*, the market for such texts was brisk. Slave narratives satisfied evangelical consciences and made vivid the drama of American freedom. Readers responded in droves, helping to establish what Theodore Parker famously called America's first truly "indigenous literature."[1]

The much-surveyed history of African American slave narratives in the literary marketplace is not, however, my focus here. Rather, I want to look beyond the implications of literacy to consider what slave narratives can tell us about the relationships between authorship and popular memory, the book as text and the book as work. Among the nineteenth-century

African American authors who made a living through print culture, there is one who questioned literacy while also capitalizing on it: Sojourner Truth, who was uniquely positioned to understand that the book's true power lies in its ability to produce memories and thus history.

Sojourner Truth's Critical Revision

If we apply standard definitions of authorship, we must say that Sojourner Truth, an illiterate former slave, left no written record of her own. Yet during and after her lifetime, Truth's publications forged an iconic identity in a print-laden world. Chief among these publications were the *cartes de visite* she sold to her supporters. Emblazoned with the slogan "I Sell the Shadow to Support the Substance," Truth's photographs remain the most stable record of her efforts to intervene in a culture that had shifted from speech to writing and from image to text. Reading these pictures in light of the uses to which she put them offers us a glimpse into Truth's self-fashioning that is unlike any other record of her life and career. What might seem ephemeral photographic evidence in fact exposes the hand of the author and reveals the deliberately unwritten story of Truth's greatest accomplishment: establishing herself as a historical entity and international icon. My analysis of her representational legacy braids together two strands of theoretical thinking: one that has taken shape around visual culture and one that has focused on materiality and the history of the book.

By the time Truth began carefully constructing her visual image, she had already experienced the complexity of print culture. Although her own narrative appeared in 1850, her fame stems from a speech she made at an 1851 women's rights rally in Akron, Ohio. The print history of this speech—popularly known as "Ar'n't I a Woman?" or "Ain't I a Woman?"—epitomizes the difficulty scholars have faced in pinning down its charismatic author. The speech exists in two versions that bear little resemblance to each other, casting doubt on its value as an authentic source. Yet its circulation and redactions have played a critical role in the indelible etching of Truth's image in public memory. Indeed, the long life and afterlife of that image, I believe, have as much to do with the instability of its record as with her remarkable manipulation thereof. Truth was interested in how text can forge memory, not the material remnants of text.

Where Jane Johnston Schoolcraft's bilinguality helped us pry apart the link between literacy and culture, Truth's archive—oral and visual, as well as textual—helps us redefine the importance of the literary in literary history. In the context of her developing reputation, the 1851 speech and the 1864 *cartes de visite* are much more than reactions against white culture's production of her image. If we review her archive through the protocols of speech and image, rather than writing and print, we can see how Truth's purposeful reliance on a collaborative form of authorship allowed her to operate with radical independence outside the confines of a static, single-authored text.[2]

Truth understood collaboration not just as a relationship but as a material act, in forms such as reprinting, and an iterative process, as when others created media that she had initially arranged and composed. As an "author," then, she anticipates the fundamental changes in publication and information circulation of the twenty-first-century digital media environment. Circulating letters to the editor, speeches, photographs, and printed books through formal and informal networks, Truth developed her public identity through a sophisticated sense of audience engagement that strikingly resembles today's emerging social media models. She understood and made use of a notion of participatory culture long before the term came into existence. Her own biggest fan, she created a fan culture that has endured beyond her lifetime to the present moment.

The story of Sojourner Truth's refashioning of conventional print culture begins with the portrait she chose in 1850 for the frontispiece of *The Narrative of Sojourner Truth* (fig. 3). The portrait makes no secret of its mediated state. The quality of the image, with its crosshatches and carefully impressed lines, calls attention to the artistic efforts that created it, emphatically registering its status as made. It also makes conspicuous use of the mythic iconography later popularized in publications of the "Ar'n't I a Woman?" speech. The white head wrap, for instance, which became a defining part of her image, references her African past and connects her to Southern plantation slavery.[3] Like the Southern dialect in one published version of her speech, this association was in her best interest marketwise: such coded references to the South identified her as a former slave and at the same time located slavery in the South, which avoided offending Northern abolitionists. In creating the impression of the personal self through the use of public signifiers, Truth managed her image

Figure 3. Frontispiece from the 1850 edition of *The Narrative of Sojourner Truth.* Image courtesy of Documenting the American South, The University of North Carolina at Chapel Hill Libraries.

without relinquishing control over her privacy. Unlike Schoolcraft, who achieved privacy by restricting access, Truth facilitated privacy through publicity.[4]

The placement of the portrait before the title page establishes readers as viewers before they even encounter text, and thus reflects Truth's radical resistance to literacy. Though Truth used print for a variety of purposes, she remained an ardent proponent of orality, believing that letters might somehow corrupt her unmediated relationship to the "Word" as spoken and heard.[5] She is known to have ridiculed Frederick Douglass for his pursuit of literacy. When she asked, "Is God dead, Frederick?" she cleverly connected his association with print culture with his failed evangelicalism, overpowering his book knowledge and asserting her superior command of the "Word" as spoken, simply by speaking.

Truth's preference for orality reveals her anxiety about the way written language accumulates meaning and, as Walter Ong has observed, restructures consciousness.[6] She preferred to have children read to her from the Bible, because adults tended to intermingle "ideas and suppositions of their own" with the sacred text as they read, threatening its authority and risking distortion. The *Narrative* uses this example as "one among the many proofs of her energy and independence of character," but it also provides evidence of her philosophy of language.[7]

Truth clearly believed that text is negotiated through its reader, and the act of reading becomes a form of response that shapes the text in uncontrollable ways; here she anticipates the contributions of reader response criticism to our understanding of texts and their circulation. For Truth, speech and the photographic image, both of which require presence, allow the speaker and subject greater agency than text does its author. As her amanuensis Olive Gilbert observes in the *Narrative*, referring to Truth by her given name, "The impressions made by Isabella on her auditors, when moved to lofty or deep feeling, can never be transmitted to paper (to use the words of another), till by some Daguerrian art, we are enabled to transfer the look, the gesture, the tones of voice, in connection with the quaint, yet fit expressions used, and the spirit-stirring animation that, at such a time, pervades all she says."[8] Printed words cannot adequately render Sojourner Truth's message because they lack specific indication of *her*. The fullness of her speech *as spoken* defies the codified representation of text. Similarly, in greeting her readers in a portrait at the start of her *Narrative*, Truth only approximates her physical presence. The image, like the transcribed speech, represents the body, but is itself an interpretation. The portrait seems to suggest that this text transcribes and interprets Sojourner Truth according to very specific rules of mediation inscribed by race, class, gender, and region. The portrait risks disqualifying Truth as a subject because it radically reinforces her status as an object, albeit one to be remembered. But Truth was not one to disaggregate the seemingly competing forms of text and image; rather, she understood them as both overlapping and also discontinuous forms.[9] By yoking the portrait with the *Narrative*, she takes full advantage of the multivalent properties of image and text, speech and writing, showing a remarkable command of each form's multiple literacies.

The way the 1850 edition calls attention to the mechanical—and intrinsically faulty—nature of writing is crucial to the warping effect of image and text, speech and writing. A "Note" facing the opening page of the *Narrative* cautions readers: "It is due to the lady by whom the following Narrative was kindly written, to state, that she has not been able to see a single proof-sheet of it; consequently, it is very possible that divers errors in printing may have occurred (though it is hoped none materially affecting the sense), especially in regard to the names of individuals referred to therein. The name of Van Wagener should read Van Wagenen."[10] Distinguishing between the *Narrative*'s subject, writer, and printer, the note emphasizes the slippery process of transforming speech into writing into published book. Though "errata" were common, Truth flouts the sincerity of the form through this one's content. The note suggests that the written text goes beyond what Jean Baudrillard has famously called "a simulation"; it so lacks a referent that a proper name may (or may not) be misspelled and thus misnamed.[11] The note so vividly indicts writing and print as unstable, suspect, and utterly unreliable that we can almost hear Sojourner Truth laughing. Her agency—rather than her authority—remains uncontested.

Harriet Beecher Stowe's 1863 article on Sojourner Truth endorses the same racial stereotypes that characterize the 1850 frontispiece portrait. Stowe's essay would have been especially valuable for Truth's self-promotion, given that it was written by the author of *Uncle Tom's Cabin* and published in one of the most important literary venues of the time, the *Atlantic Monthly*. Stowe titled the article "The Libyan Sibyl," casting Truth as the powerful oracle, who is not a modern-day Cassandra but rather a down-home sage whom William Wetmore Story would later idealize in his statue of the same name.

While Stowe paints a flattering portrait of Truth's larger-than-life personality, she achieves her effect in part by promoting several myths, including the notion that Truth was born in Africa.[12] In turn, Truth becomes the occasion for Stowe to generalize about the "African race," which she does repeatedly throughout the essay: "The African seems to seize on the tropical fervor and luxuriance of Scripture imagery as something native; he appears to feel himself to be of the same blood with those old burning, simple souls, the patriarchs, prophets, and seers, whose impassioned words seem only grafted as foreign plants on the cooler stock of the occidental mind."[13] Stowe's central aim is to show the dignity of the race through its darkest and most uneducated representative.[14] Standing in metonymically for the Southern plantation slave, Truth, the dark-skinned, illiterate former slave, nicely fits the bill.

Frances Gage's rendition of Sojourner Truth's 1851 Akron speech serves these very same political purposes. Stowe suggests that if Truth had "the same culture," she might have "spoken words as eloquent and undying as those of the African Saint Augustine or Tertullian."[15] The slippage here is remarkable, for as Stowe's assertions show, Truth's spoken words are eloquent, but without the ability to write them down, their record is faulty. She thus marks a distinction between the speech act and its record that print erases in its materiality.[16] Gage's transcription of the speech has Truth speaking a crude form of Southern dialect.[17] The speech begins: "Well Chilern, whar dar is so much racket dar must be something out o' kilter. I tink dat 'twixt de niggers of de Souf and de women at de Norf all a talkin' bout rights, the men will be in a fix pretty soon." This opening sentence is characteristic of what follows: the speech is littered with references to "de Souf," "de Norf," and "de niggers." Yet Truth was not from the South and did not speak Southern dialect. She spent her slavery years in upstate New York, and her first language was Dutch. Gage's use of Southern dialect clearly denotes *racial* rather than regional affiliation. The famous repeated rhetorical question "Ar'n't I a woman?" (which in Gage's text actually reads "A'n't I a woman?") also appears to have been an editorial flourish, which is to say an outright fabrication.[18]

Yet despite its inauthenticity, it is difficult to part with Gage's version of the speech because of what Henry Jenkins and his co-authors call its "spreadability."[19] No matter how you spell it the phrase "Ain't I a woman" has kept Sojourner Truth in the public eye, helped make her an icon, and garnered its own life well beyond its supposed originator. Of twenty images gathered from a Google search using this tag line, only a small fraction picture Truth the woman; the rest register the generative power of the phrase. There is no need, however, to reject the speech as evidence of Truth's artistry, because Truth herself took ownership of it. In reprinting Gage's version in her 1875 *Narrative*, Truth claims the words as her own, once again baffling traditional definitions of authorship. We can see this claim, or reprinting, as akin to today's reblogging (on Tumblr), retweeting (on Twitter), and sharing (on Facebook) of material that others produce but we ourselves authorized.

A decade before she adopted Gage's words as her own, Truth entered the interpretive fray to modify her existing image herself. In 1864, having already made a name for herself as a speaker in women's rights and abolitionist circles, Truth branched out into another highly scripted line of business: *cartes de visite.* Dressed in the garb of Quaker womanhood, Truth posed for the camera numerous times, arranging and perfecting her image according to the visual codes of the period. Her effort was justified, for the sale of the *cartes de visite* became one of her primary means of financial support (along with the speaking engagements at which she sold the *Narrative*).[20]

The image in figure 4 was Truth's favorite. It traffics in all the stereotypes of middle-class white womanhood, in contrast to the image of the outspoken woman who exposed her breast to prove she was a woman at the request of an audience member.[21] The knitting, book, and flowers are particular visual signifiers of nineteenth-century genteel domestic femininity. One scholar even suggests that Truth deliberately placed light shawl against dark homespun to make it difficult to date the photograph precisely, thus extending its market "shelf life."[22]

Although this image remains well known today, little has been done to put it into the context of Truth's life and publication history. By the time she visited the photographers James J. and Croydon Chandler Randall in Detroit, Truth had garnered substantial public attention from Gage's rendition of her speech and Stowe's article. The wave of renewed interest in all things abolitionist put in motion by the Emancipation Proclamation surely added to that attention. But perhaps more significantly, this set of photographs should be seen as Truth's active response to the way others were solidifying her own image around her.

The success of her intervention relies on her own canny understanding of how nineteenth-century viewers understood the relationship between the subject and its photographic representation. Roland Barthes identifies the peculiar power of the photographic image, arguing that a photograph is "somehow co-natural with its referent": it retains a level of presence absent in other referential systems. Indeed, as a signifier, the photograph documents "the necessarily real thing which has been placed

Figure 4. One of Truth's favorite *cartes de visite*, unidentified photographer, 1864. Image courtesy of Library of Congress, Prints and Photographs Division. LC-DIGppmsca-08978.

before the lens."[23] The photograph allows Truth to preserve her presence long after her speech has ended, retaining a place in the imagination of her listeners as they return to the world of readers. Barthes's reflections resonate even more deeply when we recall how the limitations of the 1850 portrait frontispiece replicated the strictures placed on her authorial control of print conventions. In contrast, photography and the *carte de visite* gave her access to a broader array of expressive techniques.

Not only did Truth control her visual image in her *cartes de visite*, she also challenged the standard practices of photographers by using copyright conventions derived from print publication to protect her image and maximize her profits. Photographers typically held the copyright to images produced in their studios. Truth subverted this system informally by printing her slogan on the front of the *cartes de visite*, thus calling attention to her ownership. Perhaps more significantly, she entered her image into copyright under her own name as early as 1864 in the Eastern District of Michigan.[24] Truth aggressively marketed these images through letters penned by her grandson published in papers such as the *Anti-Slavery Bugle*. The letters acted as a do-it-yourself marketing campaign by announcing their availability, cost, and purchase information. All in all, Truth's command of her image through her active use of iconography, legal protection, and marketing exposes her various roles as artful purveyor, producer, and product of her legacy.

These seemingly disparate elements of self-promotion come together as a form of self-production in the 1875 edition of Truth's *Narrative*. This edition, which Nell Painter considers the closest thing we have to an "authorized biography," is the last one Truth collaborated on before her death in 1878. Upon opening the book, in place of the frontispiece portrait found in earlier editions, the reader encounters an engraving based on one of the 1864 *cartes de visite* (fig. 5). Truth was photographed in at least seven separate poses at this sitting, suggesting a degree of intentional craft and artful manipulation in what might seem a stereotypical portrait of the era.[25] As noted earlier, however, part of Truth's success rested on her routine retooling of convention to suit her purposes.

The shift from a portrait to an image based on a photograph accomplished several things. For one, the photograph she used is the only image of Truth smiling. The etching engages viewers with her kindly smile, in contrast to the rigid pose and accusatory glance of the earlier portrait. Its origin as a known photograph also corrects the earlier frontispiece by directly referencing Truth's actual existence.[26] Truth's headdress is transformed from a turban to a Quaker bonnet, which, in combination with the shawl and homespun cloth of the simple gown, presents the author as dignified, if not a little antique, rather than as the exotic African/slave. The image thus also picks up on changes made to the title page (fig. 6). Unlike earlier editions, this one no longer identifies Truth as "A Northern Slave" but, in Gothic font, declares her "A bondswoman

Figure 5. Frontispiece from the 1875 edition of *The Narrative of Sojourner Truth*. Image courtesy of Documenting the American South, The University of North Carolina at Chapel Hill Libraries.

of olden times." In other words, slavery is figured rhetorically and visually as a thing of the past. Like the Gothic lettering, the terms "bondswoman" and "olden" emphasize a gentility that was categorically absent in the earlier editions. Thus we see Truth's public persona revised here in image, text, and font.

Interestingly, Truth included Stowe's "Sojourner Truth: The Libyan Sibyl" in a segment called "Book of Life," a new feature of the 1875 edition, and used Stowe's title as the caption to the frontispiece. In fact, you

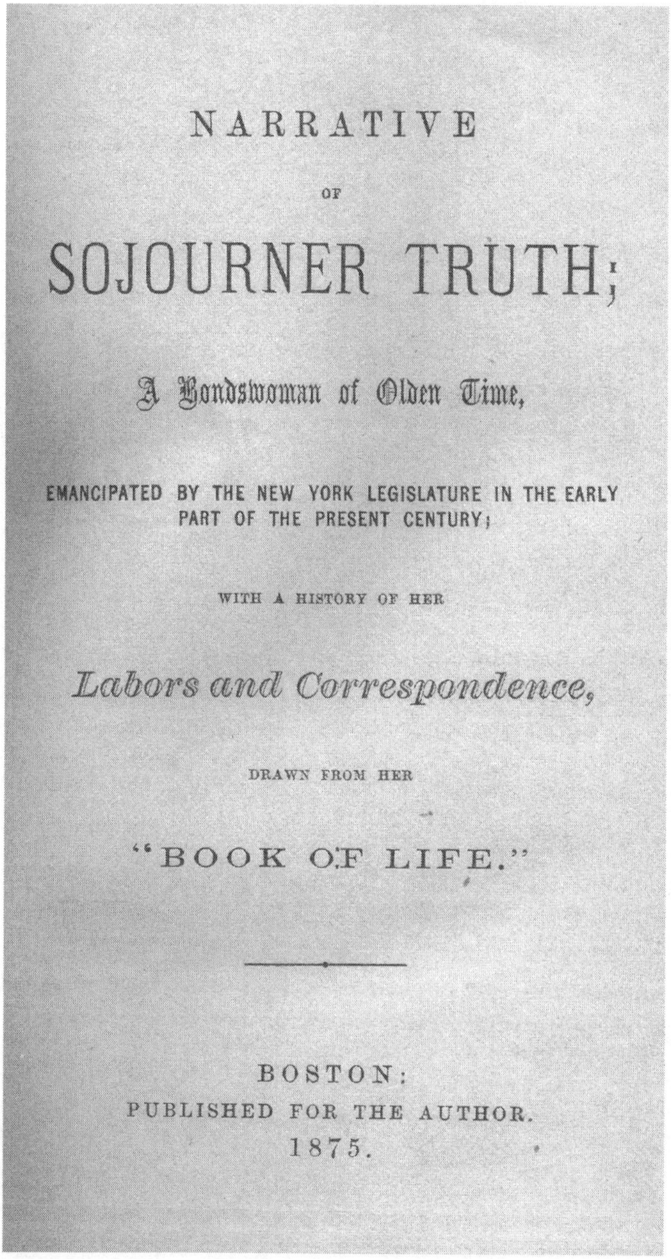

NARRATIVE

OF

SOJOURNER TRUTH;

A Bondswoman of Olden Time,

EMANCIPATED BY THE NEW YORK LEGISLATURE IN THE EARLY PART OF THE PRESENT CENTURY;

WITH A HISTORY OF HER

Labors and Correspondence,

DRAWN FROM HER

"BOOK OF LIFE."

BOSTON:
PUBLISHED FOR THE AUTHOR.
1875.

Figure 6. Title page from the 1875 edition of *The Narrative of Sojourner Truth.* Image courtesy of Documenting the American South, The University of North Carolina at Chapel Hill Libraries.

could say that Truth rebranded herself according to Stowe, replacing what had become her trademark phrase, "I sell the shadow to support the substance," with "The Libyan Sibyl" in a (self-) appropriation that adds another layer of opacity to an already difficult-to-interpret case of agency. Truth did not, however, entirely abandon the earlier frontispiece, for she made use of that engraving as the introductory image for the "Book of Life." Now serving as a frontispiece for a kind of book within a book, the image introduces readers to a set of documents that sketch a more multivalent portrait of the book's protagonist. There is, however, a slight change in the presentation of the portrait, whose caption now reads "A Picture taken in the days of her Physical Strength," surely a fiction, as no such photograph ever existed, leaving us to wonder how much agency we can assign to this image.[27]

Should this image, along with the *Narrative* and the "Book of Life," be dismissed from the archive as inauthentic or too deeply mediated? Might we, perhaps more boldly, simply dismiss it as a lie? Or should we consider the alleged photographic trace to be one more example of Truth's canny manipulation of contemporary expectations? If so, the false reference to the portrait's photographic trace matters less than the suggested importance of the photographic image, which now has precisely the same liminal (and fabulistic) status as Gage's version of Truth's speech and Stowe's portrayal of her as the Libyan Sibyl. Through the insistence on the reference, the image is inserted into the text as testimony, much like the other representations of Truth in the "Book of Life." It is certainly tempting to dismiss Gage's and Stowe's contributions as caricatures rooted in American ideas about slaves. But rather than simply jettison these representations as false or too deeply mediated by the ideologies of others, we must accept that Truth herself utilized them as authorized witnesses, legitimizing them by reprinting them in the "Book of Life," a bricolage of materials that all "testify" to her cultural standing.

Indeed, if we emphasize authorship as the construction of memory rather than the production of text, Truth is free to utilize all manner of material, regardless of its origin. She herself makes no secret of the communal act responsible for the construction of her memory. Indeed, she redefines collaboration in one more way by publishing the endorsements she has received, which serve as concluding and conclusive evidence of her worldwide reputation. In a section titled "Autographs of Distinguished Persons, WHO HAVE BEFRIENDED SOJOURNER TRUTH BY

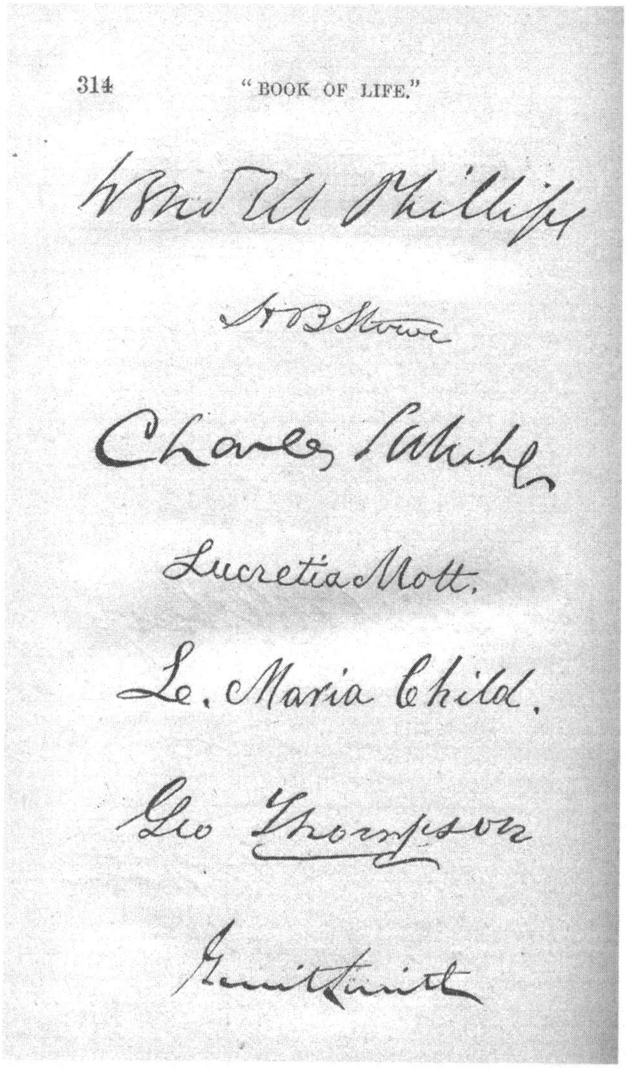

Figure 7a. Autographs from the 1875 edition of *The Narrative of Sojourner Truth.* Image courtesy of Documenting the American South, The University of North Carolina at Chapel Hill Libraries.

WORDS OF SYMPATHY AND MATERIAL AID,” readers become viewers of Sojourner Truth’s scrapbook (fig. 7a and b).

Beyond the suggestion of social intimacy, the autographs prioritize human presence over the mechanical act of textual authorship as the ultimate measure of a life and reputation.[28] Like the images discussed earlier

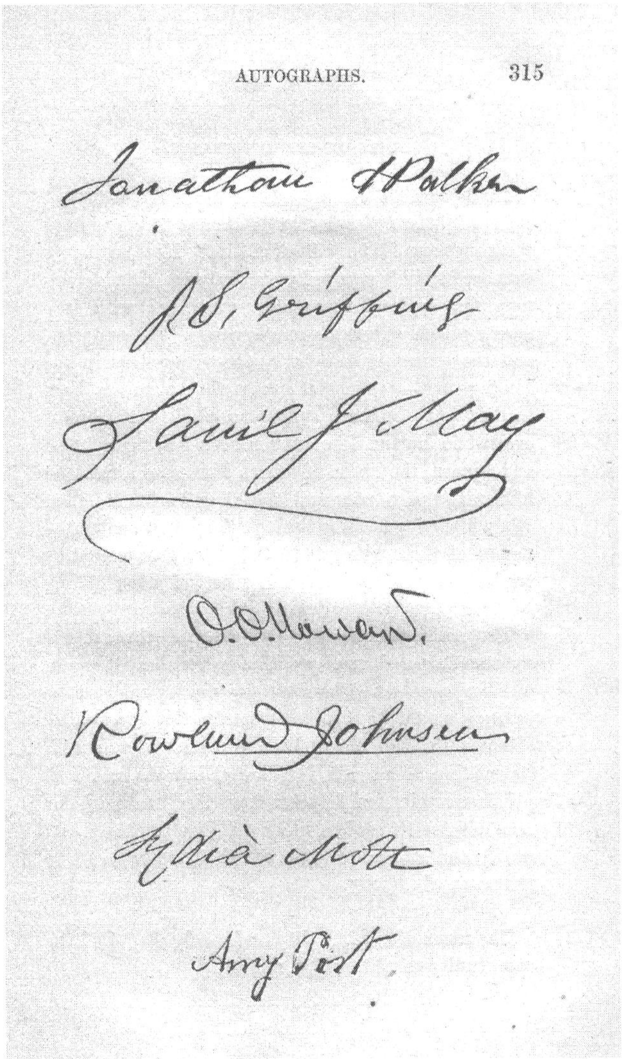

Figure 7b. More autographs from the 1875 edition of *The Narrative of Sojourner Truth.* Image courtesy of Documenting the American South, The University of North Carolina at Chapel Hill Libraries.

in this chapter, the signatures imbue Truth's text with physical presence, tapping the history of the autograph's "ability to connect its reader directly to the writer's bodily organs: hearts, eyes, brains, and especially hands" to make manifest her living fan base.[29] Appropriating their hands to herself, Truth transforms writing into image by reproducing actual signatures. Handwriting requires that we use the interpretation strategies needed to process visual images together with those demanded by printed text. "This visual dimension," as communications scholars Sonja Neef and José van Dijck observe, "distinguishes standardized mechanical writing from handwriting, which is idiosyncratic and often risks being illegible. This specific materiality qualifies the handwritten text as allographic and autographic at once; its semiotics unfold in this in-between media, as 'text-image' or as 'image-text.'"[30] Truth's manipulation of human physicality through the autograph anticipates—and complicates—the future of print culture in the digital age, when not only is all text image by virtue of code, but also text and image intersect in multimodal digital formats.

The Virtual Author Made Visible Icon

In a letter dated January 17, 1870, reprinted in the "Book of Life," Olive Gilbert, the amanuensis for Truth's 1850 *Narrative*, writes, "I did not think you were laying the foundation of such an almost world-wide reputation when I wrote that little book for you."[31] In building upon that foundation, Truth used her sophisticated sense of how to deploy key principles of orality, like testimony, within a print-laden, commodity-driven evangelical culture. Though she must have been proud of the prominence Stowe's article bestowed on her, as evidenced by its inclusion in her own "Book of Life," there was something peculiar about the piece that might have argued against its inclusion, especially in a "Book of *Life*." For Stowe spoke of Truth as if she were dead. Rather than correct her rhetorical death, however, Truth capitalized on her transformation from famous to LEGENDARY. Indeed, our own preference for textual evidence over testimony keeps her exactly that: a legend whose carefully crafted public self we recognize, but whom we never really know.

What, then, can we say about the vexed question of authorship? Remarking on the condition of Truth's legacy vis-à-vis the 1878 edition, Nell Painter observes that "with neither single author, coherent viewpoint, nor chronological order, . . . [the] editions of the *Narrative* present a fractured portrait."[32] From these fractures, and through a close study of Truth's many and various representations and self-representations, we catch a glimpse of the degree to which her authorship is constructed more blatantly than in seemingly stable single-authored texts. Truth calls attention, in some bold ways, to the interpretive space between speaking and writing, image and text, for as a black woman living in mid-nineteenth-century America, she understood the paradoxical nature of representation in ways that were both visceral and inevitable.[33]

"I am a self-made woman," Truth announced in the 1875 edition of the *Narrative*.[34] But it's important to note not just that she made a self but that she made herself through concentrated efforts to engage marketplace conventions and demands. Insofar as she *could* make herself, she did. Yet there are some disturbing implications to her story. Asked late in life why she looked so young, she explained that she had two skins, a black one covering a white one. Her racial attitudes are troubling, especially with respect to the politically charged valence of race in our time. Yet her internalized racism becomes a way for us to understand her conception of the world in which she lived. She knew that race mattered, and that as a dark-skinned black woman, she had to make race work to her advantage, so she manipulated the iconographies of race and gender in the images she used to promote and support herself. When she says she sold the shadow to support the substance, we might understand shadow to mean "race" and thus see her as a participant in the race trade that drove the market of the period.[35] Nonetheless, Truth's remixing of the conventions of visual and print cultures, rather than conforming to their rules, is one of the things that makes her exemplary. Her story grants us an unusually illuminating look into the complexities of agency within the context of visual and print culture, while also showing us how these two mediums are inextricably linked. In image and text, Truth lets her substance be seen only from behind the shadow of the racist paradigms that shaped publication opportunities for African Americans.

Sojourner Truth's representations—in their various modes and appearance—benefit from the tensions created as they bring alternate systems of meaning into contact. She plays with the idea of the photograph as an indexical sign marking the presence of the subject, while also capitalizing on the image's iconographic power to transform and transfer meaning. Truth thus anticipates Henry James's distinctive use of photography, which reveals the medium's more evocative qualities. James's use of the medium challenges the too facile alignment of photography and realism. In the photographic plates he selected for the New York Edition of his works, the viewer encounters the real—an actual location—with the least degree of realism.[36] These photographs are not there for their documentary strength, but rather to plunge readers into an interpretive quandary. They do not depict as much as they provoke, emphasizing the need to interpret mood, tone, and the other narrative challenges James poses for his readers.

Whereas James resists the demands of popular culture, Truth outwits them. As we have seen, her use of photography is perhaps even more provocative for its seeming complicity with popular forms and codes permeating nineteenth-century U.S. culture regarding race, gender, class, and region. Her use of text and composition practices over the course of her many reprintings illuminates the pitfalls of photography as it lures us into a complacent acceptance of the pose as real while it is only a medium. Truth emphasizes the constructedness of the image; she unsettles the authority of writing and print, even as she uses both to claim her presence—selling the shadow to support the substance. She grappled with forms as Jacob wrestled with the angel: in a fight for survival. Her work succeeds in teaching those of us who are entrenched in a literacy-laden print culture to think outside the book just as persistently as we struggle with it.

CHAPTER 3

History (Publication Redefined)

Jane Johnston Schoolcraft and Sojourner Truth understood that publication is a privileged form of history-making. Tracking their shrewd approaches to publication has delineated an alternate nineteenth-century literary history that anticipates twenty-first-century new media. To accomplish this tracking, however, I have relied on publication itself, with its documented processes and identifiable coordinates of people, place, and time, to verify these authors and texts as historical. In other words, in chapters 1 and 2, I use traditional scholarly methods of reconstructing the past to identify innovation in that same past. In this chapter, I reverse those terms. Rather than using scholarship and publishing history to investigate individual historically verified authors, I look directly at scholarship, publication, and authorship, taking up the theoretical questions prompted by a nineteenth-century manuscript written by a hitherto unknown author and left unpublished until 2002.

The holographic manuscript of *The Bondwoman's Narrative* by Hannah Crafts was discovered in an auction catalogue by Henry Louis Gates Jr. He purchased it on February 15, 2001. Scholars subsequently tested the hypothesis that Crafts was an African American woman and a fugitive slave. Gregg Hecimovich, a professor at Winthrop University in Rock

Hill, South Carolina, definitely identified "Hannah Crafts" as Hannah Bond—a slave woman who ultimately escaped from slavery.[1] *The Bondwoman's Narrative* now takes its place as the earliest extant text by an African American to exist in manuscript form. My interest here, however, is not in debates over identity or the importance of *The Bondwoman's Narrative* to African American literary history, but rather in the text's contribution to literary history more generally, especially in the context of publishing practices emerging in the twenty-first century. The complex ambiguity of its intertwined text, author, and editor offers us an opportunity to reconsider the meaning of publication and its role in constructing history.

As both unpublished manuscript and published literary sensation, Bond's book operates according to a programmed algorithm of race that has had an enormous effect on the outcomes of literary history. As an unpublished manuscript, unencumbered by considerations of reception, circulation, and readership, *The Bondwoman's Narrative* intensifies the value of the book as ritual artifact and cultural practice, in part because of the way publishing shaped African American authorship in the nineteenth century. As a group, African Americans had a fraught history with literacy: they were barred by law from learning to read and write during slavery and limited by custom to nonfiction narratives. *The Bondwoman's Narrative* engages intensely with literacy itself, wrestling with its complex cultural history through genre, references to canonical texts, plot mechanisms, and its own history. Bond thus plays well beyond the limits ascribed to African American authors in the mid-nineteenth century, crafting, as it were, a text that could only be published nearly 150 years later, when a valorized African American literature had long since overcome the question of African American literacy.

Using these facts about Hannah Bond and her text to consider larger issues pertaining to publication requires that we consider the limits of the author function, especially with regard to posthumous publication. In the end, the fluidity of the text and our fluid knowledge of its author increase the value of knowing what her text is and who wrote it, even as the details bring us back to two defining moments in twentieth-century literary criticism: Foucault's declaration of the end of the author and Stanley Fish's *Is There a Text in This Class?*[2] In this chapter I explore the levels of uncertainty that *The Bondwoman's Narrative* productively exploits, ultimately considering how they illuminate contemporary Web 2.0 publishing practices. At stake here are the central terms by which we establish and develop historical knowledge. As projections of literary history, Hannah Bond and her text lay bare the interdependence of publication and history, reminding us how crucial publication has long been to the making of history.

Fugitive Author / Fugitive Text

The existence of *The Bondwoman's Narrative* allows us to question what history means in literary history. Because the text remained unpublished until Gates discovered it, we cannot examine it through the usual indexical coordinates of publication. Indeed, its literary status cannot even be broached until its historical position has been established, making its materiality uniquely pertinent: without a publisher, and with an only very recently recovered author, Bond's story begins with the paper she wrote on and the ink she used, the very materials of literary production, which provide the concrete evidence that establishes the text's historical status.

Gates began here too, enlisting the help of Joe Nickell, the expert who declared the diary of Jack the Ripper a forgery.[3] Using the sophisticated tools of forensic analysis, Nickell traced the manuscript's pen, ink, paper, and handwriting to the mid-nineteenth century. He bolstered his case with internal evidence, such as a reference to an equestrian statue that did not exist before 1853. Beyond this solid factual ground, he inferred from the style of handwriting, tone, and references that the manuscript was written by a "young, African-American woman who was deeply religious."[4] Nickell's historical authentication of the manuscript opened the way for historical and literary scholars to pursue the question of Bond's actual identity and the generic classification of her text.

Both of these questions have resisted definitive answers. *The Bondwoman's Narrative* revolves around a female slave's experience of and subsequent escape from plantation slavery, marking it as a form of slave narrative. The narrative, however, almost entirely resists identifiable signifiers such as place names, an authorial choice that repudiates the conventions of the slave narrative and marks it as fiction. At the same time, it contains many references to verifiable facts and has actual historical origins: with the help of clues provided by the previous owner of the manuscript, Gates was able to identify the novel's fictionalized plantation and its owner, John Hill Wheeler. The text similarly gives up some clues as to its author, who has now been identified as a fugitive mixed-race woman. But these clues and the conclusions they suggest are as partial as they are significant.

In the case of Hannah Bond's text, authorial identity is a crucial determinant within the context of African American literary history. If *The Bondwoman's Narrative* is indeed fiction, it would also hold the honor of being the first novel written by an African American woman, preceding Harriet Wilson's *Our Nig*.[5] But although it is important to note these historical markers and their significance, much of the thinking that informed this chapter derived from the text's ambiguities, even before Bond's identity had been verified.

The hard and fast distinctions between author and narrator, nonfiction and novel crumble as we better understand the relationship between the author and her text. Hannah, the novel's protagonist, is a fugitive slave, as was Bond, its author. Research shows that *The Bondwoman's Narrative* is a mixed-genre text; it is neither strictly fact nor solely fiction. In not only escaping the confines of the slave narrative, the defining genre of slave authors, but also remaining unpublished, the book became a fugitive text.[6] As fugitives, both author and text risked oblivion to net the freedom to think outside the book.

Now that we can identify Bond without a doubt, some of the confusion between her and her text is reduced, yet its fugitive status remains. Even as scholars have had to rely on an unusual mixture of genealogical research and textual evidence to define the limits of the search for the author, they have continued to problematize the very status of author. In the process of using text as context to solve the riddle of identity, the author as historical entity and narrator as aesthetic tool fuse, as do the text as story and the text as history.

Literacy and Literary History in *The Bondwoman's Narrative*

There is no doubt about Hannah Bond's literacy and, beyond that, her literary acuity. Whereas Harriet Beecher Stowe felt compelled to verify the sources of her fiction with the 1854 publication of *A Key to Uncle Tom's Cabin*, Bond uses the reverse strategy, authenticating her literacy—and thus her validity as an author—by reference to the literary. She asserts the terms of her authorship by refusing to remain within the sanctioned racial boundaries offered by the factual narrative, leaving that literary ghetto behind as she strikes out toward the figurative freedoms of the novel, using respected white writers as her textual sources. In claiming the writing and forms of free whites as her own, she claims her own freedom and enacts the entitlement that literacy brings, remediating herself from slave to author. At the same time, her choice of genre undoubtedly played an inhibiting role in her chances for publication.[7]

John Hill Wheeler, owner of the plantation that served as one of Craft's historical sources, and with which she was certainly familiar as a slave, kept a diary and catalogued his library in 1850.[8] A catalogue for the library's sale, compiled in 1883 after Wheeler's death, provides another glimpse into the books of an upper-class Southern politician of the period, as well as an inkling of Bond's possible literary resources. For instance, collections of speeches by the British abolitionist William Wilberforce and the American slavery opponent Henry Ward Beecher, brother of Harriet Beecher Stowe, could have offered Bond a way to sound out her own thoughts about the peculiar institution.[9] While such abolitionist writings offer little insight into either Bond's selection of fiction as her mode or her specific narrative choices, the library also included fictionalized first-person narratives such as *The Banker's Wife; or, Court and City: A Novel* and *The Gambler's Wife: A Novel.*[10] According to Bryan Sinche, these books were most likely part of the parlor library; in *The Bondwoman's Narrative,* Hannah directly states that she had her pick of such volumes. This kind of fiction would have provided Bond with examples of how popular mainstream novels portrayed many of the settings that mobilize features of their plots.[11]

Bond's experiments with genre recall Schoolcraft, who also claimed authorial and textual freedom through her exercise of literacy. Her knowledge and use of the formal features of canonical writers demonstrate that Bond understood the book as text and the work text can do. Replicating generic features in circulation among white writers grants her story access to the shared sense of ritual and collective consciousness genre provides.[12] As a novel passing for an autobiography, *The Bondwoman's Narrative* calls attention to the powerful freedom fiction imparts to writers and readers to imagine and create themselves beyond the immediate and sometimes irreversible contingencies of our world. At the same time, in a testament to self-schooling, Bond's text is speckled with references to the great works of Western literature, from the Greek tragedies to Shakespeare and Byron. Her literary "samplings" suggest the interpretive communities with which she wishes to connect.[13] Inserting passages from Dickens as well as a plot line from *Bleak House*, references to Byron, and clichés popularized by classical authors such as Homer and Virgil, without clear attribution, Bond implies that she expects readers to have read the same volumes. Perhaps even more significantly, by incorporating the words of other (white) writers into her text, she puts her work on an even plane with theirs, proving her claim to literacy.

Wheeler's library also held several works by African American authors, including an 1833 edition of Phillis Wheatley's poems that appears in the catalogue made after his death. On the one hand, Wheatley's work is suggestive of Bond's relationship to white literary tradition, foreshadowing Bond's radical appropriation of white forms—and her awareness of the consequences she could expect to face if she pursued publication. On the other hand, Bond also mobilized features of the slave narrative form when they served her purposes. Beginning with its very title, *The Bondwoman's Narrative* reinforces the value of that form as a political tool and as a powerful signifier within a burgeoning antebellum market for books, where writings about slavery, even those tied in to the topic ever so loosely, sold well.[14] Oddly, however, Bond never mentions her encounters with texts by Douglass, Wheatley, or any other African American writers, nor does she include them among her literary references. Instead, we find her referencing and emulating white mainstream fiction of the sort she, like her narrator, might have encountered in the parlor library.

The Bondwoman's Narrative and the Literary

As a story, *The Bondwoman's Narrative* is chock-full of action, excitement, passion, and wrongdoing. The text begins and ends with Aunt Hetty, a kind white woman who teaches Hannah how to read at its start and reappears at its close to help her escape from slavery. Between these symmetrical bookends, the reader learns of the great and horrible labyrinth of slavery, in which characters, including Hannah's mistress (who turns out to be passing for white), are bought and sold, escape from and are returned to slavery. The sentimentally tinged slave narrative form itself enfolds tales that bear the marks of a variety of genres, including sensationalism and the gothic.[15]

A crucial indicator of the importance of literature to *The Bondwoman's Narrative* is the way in which books and reading mold the story itself. Hannah tells us, "My mistress was very kind, and unknown to Master she indulged me in reading [the books in the parlor] whenever I desired" (36). Indeed, the novel's central story is established here, on one of Hannah's forays into the library, where she sits "with a book behind the heavy damask curtains that shaded the window" (36). The sunlight enables her to read, but Hannah soon overhears another story, as outside the curtains, the novel's archvillain, the lawyer Trappe, unfolds his designs for extortion, threatening to reveal her mistress's "true" identity (45). Hannah's earlier suspicions about her mistress that "there was mystery, something indefinable about her," due as much to her physical features as to her behavior ("her lips . . . were too large, full and red" for a white woman [27]), prove well founded. The mulatto daughter of a slave woman, the new Lady of Lindendale is a slave under the law, which states that children must "follow the condition of the mother." She will be remanded to slavery if Trappe is not appeased, and this secret, uncovered by Trappe, sets the plot in motion.

As sensational as this discovery is, it is important to note that it occurs as an indirect result of Hannah's relationship to books, especially her love of a good story. Hannah's enjoyment of literature also reveals the greatest danger posed by black literacy to white culture: reading produces writing, and writing, especially black writing, presents a special threat to the budding profession of authorship, which is constituted by whites only. Though her mistress is caught in the trap laid by the villainous Trappe, Hannah escapes the nonfiction slave narrative form that traps other fugitive slave authors. If the plot of the novel turns on its narrator's quest for freedom from slavery, its publication history tells the story of freedom from the literary marketplace. Describing herself as having "a silent unobtrusive way of observing things and events," the narrator endows herself with the features of a writer (5). But readers would not know exactly what *kind* of a writer so long as the book remained in manuscript form. Writing made Bond, like her character, an author, while *not* publishing kept her free.

But if Bond freed herself from the literary marketplace, she remained firmly embedded within the literary itself, albeit on her own terms. Within the generic containers noted earlier, she demonstrates her imagined and imaginative freedom, as she and her mistress make their escape, by treating her readers to an unusual degree of social and psychological realism. Rather than dwell, like most slave narrators, on the verifiable facts, Hannah declares, "I cannot describe my journey; the details would be dry, tedious, uninteresting." Instead, she unsparingly depicts the suffering she and her mistress experience during their flight from slavery, heightening the sense of emotional and physical discomfort. A hut offers shelter but reeks from a moldy heap of straw (66). The food they gather is paltry (66). Their bodies, worn out from the strenuous journey, appear weak, their clothing torn (67). When they approach others, the threat of danger is palpable (56). In these scenes and throughout the whole narrative, Bond is deeply interested in conveying the psychological and social experiences of slavery, forging her brand of humanitarian realism.[16] Anticipating Zora Neale Hurston's argument, in "What White Publishers Won't Print," that African American writers should delve into the psychological realm of their characters to foster realism and dimensionality, Bond makes the mood and physical condition of her characters central to her story.

Slave narratives also have an oblique effect on *The Bondwoman's Narrative* through the impact of publication on the lives of those who went into print as authors and fugitive slaves, which Bond surely noted. She may also have learned about the dangers of public recognition that accompany celebrity status from the experience of a fellow slave in Wheeler's household. Jane Johnson became a cause célèbre when she and her two sons escaped from her master on a trip to Philadelphia, assisted by Passmore Williamson, secretary of the Pennsylvania Abolition Society, who was subsequently arrested for forcibly interfering with Wheeler's attempt to prevent the escape.[17] Picked up by several major newspapers, including the *New York Tribune*, the *Philadelphia Ledger*, and the *New Orleans Times-Picayune*, the story also appeared in pamphlet form and was later recounted in an 1872 book, *The Underground Railroad*.[18] These publications, it turns out, authorize Bond's novel in unusual ways.

The Bondwoman's Narrative suggests that Jane Johnson's escape made way for Bond to become a lady's maid. But Johnson's notoriety may also have had on impact on what Bond left out of the novel. Adjuring her readers to imagine Hannah's freedom at the novel's close denies them the details and emotional gratification they crave. But silence on life after slavery is a necessary condition for a freedom untrammeled by capital, the market, and possibly a return to slavery.[19] It also prevents the text from becoming a production of capital, instead enabling it to protect its own aesthetic project from the vicissitudes of the market. Publication would bring publicity and circulate Bond's portrait, like Jane Johnson's and Passmore Williamson's, among the newspapers and drawing rooms of the day.[20] Safe freedom, for the fugitive slave, means remaining unread.

If slave narratives both shaped *The Bondwoman's Narrative* and provided a model from which to deviate, Bond also borrowed serial writing strategies from the novel, lacing her text with cues that its story is of the "to-be-continued" variety. Introducing the plotline of the Northern white couple who teach Hannah to read, she writes, "Years passed, however, before I learned their fate," signaling their eventual return in her imagined reader's mind (13). Suturing her tale with such cliffhangers, Bond breaks up the narrative into installments designed to move the reader forward and connect its disparate "episodes." She may actually have intended to serialize the piece, though it seems more likely that she was responding to the literary influence of Dickens.[21] Although some have deemed her implied serial format clumsy, it registers her aesthetic project: to write a novel, not a nonfiction narrative.[22]

The serial installment builds reader interest, but it also creates a particular understanding of time and its relationship to history. Philosophically, the serial posits that history continues but does not repeat itself. Its lesson is that consequences may be slow in coming, but they never fail to arrive. The form thus encourages those who have been disenfranchised historically to expect justice in the end. Reappearing characters help shape Bond's iteration of this particular conception of history, which is deeply connected to the history of slavery. Treating history as a continuous series of events linked ever so slightly by coincidence, she finds ways to uncover cause-and-effect relationships and thus apportion blame and responsibility in what might otherwise seem haphazard incidents.[23]

The chapter "Lindendale," named after the plantation at which it takes place, exhibits the serial's ability to bring the past to bear on the present. Although the chapter initially seems to be a story about ancestry and tradition, its embedded tale of family portraits takes readers into a gothic world of pain and suffering, where tradition mutates into a horrible legacy revisited on the family, much in the tradition of Edgar Allan Poe. Sir Clifford, the patriarch of Lindendale, proclaims that all future members of the family, by blood or marriage, must display their portraits in the ancestral hall. Privileging an aristocratic model of power by emphasizing "family," Sir Clifford's edict stresses family as spectacle, the site of neither nurturing nor love, but rather a vehicle for handing down power in the form of property in general and slaves in particular. Like Poe in "The Fall of the House of Usher," Bond uses family history here to limn a larger story about how the sins of the fathers are visited on the sons.[24]

More significant than the gothic details of the portraits themselves is the effect of Hannah's narrative perspective on them. In the gallery, we first experience this effect as Hannah's point of view on mainstream Anglo-American history. When she describes how the portraits change as she looks at them, her viewpoint prefigures the ideological divide between black and white. Under her (literal and figurative) gaze, these former masters lose their stately presence and become hideous and terrifying, their faces morphing into monstrous self-parodies. A Poe-like tomb of the undead rather than a majestic tribute to ancestors, the gallery becomes a chamber of horrors for the narrator—and, ultimately, for everyone else in the story. Here, as elsewhere in the novel, a slave's perspective provides a wholly different outlook, representing the other side of history.

Indeed, Bond's effective representation of the slave's perspective is one of the crucial factors that pointed to the novel's author as African American, in particular, those chapters that document Hannah's recognition of the power she has not merely to frame experience but to determine it. Early in the novel, Hannah explains that she has no interest in romance since marriage is a civil right denied her as a slave. Rather than fall in love and have a family she might lose at her master's whim, she chooses to remain single as long as she is enslaved.[25] Her clear-sighted reckoning of the risks of slavery help her to identify Trappe as a trap indeed at the novel's first social event, a celebration of the master's recent wedding, on which Hannah has a less than celebratory perspective, noting, "The bridegroom was probably too happy, and the company too gay" (28). As an outsider who waits on the marriage table, rather than falling for its seductive air, she can see things others miss. Despite the fact that Trappe is "an old fashioned gentleman," hardly likely to attract attention, Hannah has "eyes and ears for only" him (27), able to see through him because of her position and her categorical refusal of romance, and of marriage as romance's ritual outcome. Thanks to her ability to read against the grain, we are introduced to the story's central villain, an unseen enemy wearing the costume of respectability, a costume Hannah immediately recognizes as not simply shabby but utterly lacking in dignity.

From the standpoint of the novel's aesthetic project, Bond's portrayal of the transformative vision of race benefits from the serial format. Bond returns to the episodic form in the chapters "Lizzy's Story" and "Lizzy's Story Continued." Lizzy's story of the Lindendale plantation is a lurid one about the return of the repressed, told by a character who was left behind when Hannah and her mistress escaped the plantation. Ushering Lizzy back into the novel suggests that there is something about her that makes her the ideal narrator for these events. Earlier in the novel, she is treated as a laughable character who takes pride in her white ancestry. Hannah tells us:

> Lizzy was much better educated than I was, and had been to many places that I had never even heard tell of. She had also a great memory for dates and names which I invariably forgot. She was a Quadroon, almost white, with delicate hands and feet, and a person that any lady in the land might have been proud of. She came, she said, of good family and frequently mentioned great names in connection with her own, and when I smiled and said it mattered little she would assume an air of consequential dignity, and assert that on the contrary it was a very great thing and very important even to a slave to be well connected—that good blood was an inheritance to them—and that they heard the name of some honorable gentleman mentioned with applause. . . . And then I said "Of course" which mollified her rumpled vanity. (33–34)

Though the reader recognizes that "of course" really means "of course not," Hannah's expert use of the phrase creates the comfort Lizzy needs to be a useful tool in her story. Of all the African American characters in the novel, Lizzy is the one who best demonstrates the hypocrisy of racial pride. When

Hannah smooths over Lizzy's "rumpled vanity" with a lie, she lets the reader know that she thinks Lizzy's affiliation with whiteness is sheer foolishness. But she also tells us that Lizzy had "a great memory for dates and names," an important feature for a tale of "unvarnished facts," especially because Hannah, as she admits here, lacks this capacity. Thus, through a complex series of rhetorical shifts, Hannah puts forward her substitute narrator as one with a better capacity for relating fact, while affirming herself as the fiction writer who knows what to say for effect rather than verification. In other words, Lizzy is the mere chronicler, while Hannah is the historian whose interpretation of facts becomes history.

At the close of chapter 13, Hannah is again hidden, this time with Lizzy, "behind some piles of lumber where" they "could be effectively screened from observation" (171). As the gothic account of sexual license among the planter class unfolds in this tale within a tale, Hannah sanitizes herself against it by not telling it herself. But why might this tale of sexual misconduct and marital infidelity invite an act of narrative ventriloquism? Lizzy's story of the Cosgroves, the residents of Lindendale, lays bare any pretensions about the physical, mental, and moral superiority of white people, revealing master and mistress to be savage, petty, and immoral. But perhaps most significantly, the story-within-a-story device gives Bond extra leeway for a scathing critique of the moral lapses made possible by slavery, particularly emphasizing their effect on women. The story condemns Mr. Cosgrove for his licentious behavior with female slaves and for betraying his wife by keeping several black mistresses. But the sex is not as egregious as the disloyalty. Mr. Cosgrove has started an alternate family with a slave woman, whom he stashes in a secret recess of the house to hide her and their children from his wife. With this story, Bond comments on an arrangement already made famous by William Wells Brown's *Clotel* (1853). Locating the mistress and her children in the house metaphorically suggests the degree to which the home has internalized slavery's corruption. Like a hidden cancer, this arrangement leads to the moral downfall of all concerned—and even death for some of the characters. No one is safe from the effects of slavery.

But putting the story in Lizzy's mouth is not enough distance for Bond. Using a tradition as old as Chaucer and Boccaccio, in Lizzy's story Bond casts Mrs. Cosgrove as an aristocratic British woman, not an American. Assuaging herself with the false notion that she has "freed" a slave, this foreign-born mistress turns the young mother and her twin babies out of the house to fend for themselves. While they face certain death from exposure, the "lady" lies upon her satin sheets eating toasted biscuits with honey. As one of only two narrative digressions in the novel, this story calls attention to itself as an emblem of narrative resistance, important in part for what it doesn't tell us. Though the tale's narrative distance is remarkable, its message is even more striking. Depicting Mrs. Cosgrove as a frustrated and infertile woman, Bond contrasts her childlessness to the fertility of the slave woman whom she sees as her de facto rival. Not only has her husband's mistress borne him two sons, but also they are twins, an unmistakable sign of the couple's fecundity. The Lady of Lindendale cannot bear the prospect that fertility and the future lie with the African American characters.

Bond's refusal to let Hannah tell this story seems as shrewd as Hannah's refusal to marry while in slavery. Hannah judiciously safeguards her literary offspring by recounting only those events to which she is an eyewitness. The novel can return to Lindendale via Lizzy's tale, while Hannah, unlike the novel's whites, who are tethered to a past that "haunts" them, remains safely within the confines of her own story, which is progressive and forward-looking.[26] Lizzy's tale emphasizes the legacy of slavery, which, far from being a symbol of white superiority and a boon to white economic power, is responsible for the downward spiral of the heirs of Lindendale. As if to underscore the tale's importance, Bond hands it over to the one black character who is both the verifiable slave narrator white readers expect and an advocate for the racial stereotypes many of the most liberal abolitionists believed.[27] In so doing, she turns literary and social mores to her own ends.

Un/Re-making History

History gives us several important clues as to why Hannah Bond did not attempt to publish her novel. Unlike Harriet Jacobs and many other African American writers of the era, she does not make a plea for financial support in her preface. She does wonder about her reception, however, in terms that suggest familiarity with the literary marketplace: "How will such a literary venture, coming from a sphere so humble, be received?" (3). Though calling the novel a "venture" might imply a business interest,

Bond never connects writing with financial need.[28] Her silence on remuneration suggests that financial aid was not a motivating factor for her writing, keeping the focus instead on her aesthetic project. Breaking away from the slave narrative's mendicant origins, Bond emphasizes her craft rather than the protocols of black authorship.[29] At the same time, the preface holds on to the most popular literary conventions of the nonfiction narrative, starting with the claim that the novel is a "record of plain unvarnished facts" (3).[30] From her avowal that the novel will appeal to "those who regard truth as stranger than fiction" to her evocation of Providence as muse, Bond demonstrates a canny understanding of the literary marketplace she rejects.[31] Modeling her fiction on nonfiction conventions, Bond seems to have anticipated the functioning algorithm of race with regard to genre. Judging from Harriet Jacobs's Pyrrhic victory in the literary marketplace—she died unknown as an author—no market existed for African American *fiction*.[32]

Enter Henry Louis Gates Jr., director of the W. E. B. Du Bois Institute at Harvard University and, perhaps more important, the scholar who brought to light the first important text written by an African American woman in the nineteenth century, Harriet Wilson's *Our Nig*. Gates's own history, in other words, helps establish and legitimize Bond's history. Indeed, in some sense, the man *People* magazine christened "the Sherlock Holmes of Black Studies" made Bond not just an author but an *African American* author.[33] As a superhero of African American literature and culture, Gates has spent his career not simply rescuing African American literature from the forgotten past but building its future. In addition to the important recovery of Wilson's novel, Gates established a monumental publishing project, the Schomburg Library of Nineteenth-Century Black Women Writers, initiated in 1988. It vies with Ticknor and Fields's prestigious nineteenth-century "blue and gold" series, which boasted titles by the major canonical American authors, including Emerson, Hawthorne, Thoreau, and Twain.[34] And like Ticknor and Fields, Gates used this distinctive series to create a pantheon of writers whose importance is underscored through the reliquary of print and the material form of the book, only his pantheon is African American and female.[35]

Leveraging his considerable clout to establish the authenticity and historical gravitas of *The Bondwoman's Narrative*, Gates enabled the text to garner readers and supporters, which in turn intensified its validity as a historical relic. The published text reaffirms the importance of the expert and the book, just as those paradigms have come under assault. Its success—it has sold well over 200,000 copies—required the forceful combination of the curatorial functions of editor, scholar, and publisher and has significant political implications: the discovery and publication of the manuscript reinscribed publication as the sine qua non of writing history. Bond, her text, and its publication history also reaffirm the importance of the embodied author, revealing how, even in a Web-based, twenty-four-hour, status-update, self-publication culture, publication still relies on identity, despite literary scholarship's disavowal thereof. At the same time, Bond exposes the limits of e-publishing today just as clearly as she reflects the restrictive publishing practices of the nineteenth century. Ultimately, in the twenty-first century, Bond's (formerly) fugitive text challenges the very conceptions of digital culture and its implied defiance of materiality, as well as the very conceptions of postmodern literary scholarship and its explicit defiance of identity, confirming the role of the book and the author in understanding literary culture as a historical projection.

Bond certainly remains mysterious, keeping us guessing by C/crafting multiple identities—as character and author, shadow and substance—that reflect further on questions about authorship and memory that were a central focus of chapter 2.[36] Yet, rather than allowing the mystery to erase text or author, we might recognize the degree to which both have been invented by the various forces that have shaped them. Both Bond and *The Bondwoman's Narrative* are the product of multiple imaginations—not just her own but those of readers, critics, historians, and scholars. Typographically, then, we might represent her text's particular status by extending the use of titular italics to include the author's name. Referring to the book as *The Bondwoman's Narrative by Hannah Crafts* indicates the degree of aesthetic and historical invention the text has required to become what it is.

For a text that existed only in manuscript form, however, readers may think of Dickinson as a more apt comparison than Harriet Wilson. Dickinson eschewed publication rather than operate according to its norms. Instead, she composed and left behind in manuscript form her fascicles—little book-like arrangements that provide evidence of her remarkable aesthetic vision and artistic integrity. Like Dickinson, Bond resisted publication in order to retain control over her aesthetic and produce the novel that today's reader can appreciate on its own terms. Even more so than in the case of other recovered texts and authors, we come to this author and her text conditioned by the excitement the discovery generated. Dubbing the novel "history-in-the-waiting," Gates correctly foresaw its remarkable appeal to today's audience.[37] In addition to the print run, Tom Cruise's production company optioned the novel and the story of its discovery for an HBO movie. These various iterations of the book affect its status as a novel and Bond's status as its author, permanently transforming both into contemporary-generated historical relics, making authorship a shared—and historically defined—position. But if the current emphasis lies on what the author and her book mean as historical entities, her own focus on her story as aesthetic object slips away.

The fate of *The Bondwoman's Narrative* also points to the role that publicity plays in the refashioning of literary history. As Gates said of the first reprinting of Wilson's *Our Nig* in 1982, "the *New York Times* made that novel."[38] The newspaper reported that Gates, at the time a young assistant professor at Yale and recent recipient of a MacArthur Foundation "genius grant," had discovered a hitherto forgotten novel by and about an African American woman. The novel appeared just as the academy and the public were seeking to create a more inclusive, "multicultural" literary history, as epitomized by the 1989 publication of the *Heath Anthology of American Literature.* In this context, Wilson's identity as an African American female author made her novel an immediate media sensation.

Wilson provides an instructive counterpoint to Bond, for we gain a glimpse of what happened upon the 1859 publication of *Our Nig.* The work of Barbara White and Eric Gardener reveals the first edition's small circulation and the novel's eclipse at the margins of literary history.[39] Without the connections to the literary culture machine that Harriet Jacobs and Frederick Douglass enjoyed, Wilson's efforts to rescue her son by writing and publishing *Our Nig* failed miserably. She died soon after its publication, and her book faded away.[40]

One key difference between Wilson and Bond, however, is that Wilson's novel was published, and Wilson's identity was known when it was published. By contrast, with so little available information about Hannah Bond at the time of the *Narrative*'s publication, those who have "authorized" her text by authenticating and publishing it have essentially, historically and conceptually, become her co-authors. Though Gates vigorously refused that appellation when asked about his role in bringing Bond's novel to light, I would argue that the title "editor" does not accurately describe his importance to this endeavor, even when understood in the sense of one who preserves the past in order to cultivate a particular vision of it.[41] Given that Gates is his own "brand," with several PBS series under his belt alongside his academic career, his endorsement of the novel, and the other scholarly endorsements he was able to obtain, made it a media sensation. In some sense, then, his editorial efforts serve as a palimpsest upon which Bond's novel is written: his story imbues hers with the cultural power she lacked in her own lifetime. Peeling away this layer reveals the text below.

From the fate of *Our Nig*, we can surmise that *The Bondwoman's Narrative* would not have fared nearly so well had it been published 150 years earlier. Gates's support, and his identification of the story as a novel, transformed it from an aesthetic project that had languished unread in the archives to a historical relic of African American literature and culture. Like other relics, the novel has been infused with an extra-aesthetic quality that far exceeds the ordinary rewards and conditions of publication. Its publication has revised the historical record in multiple dimensions: as one reviewer remarks, "The significance of the book does not rest on its primacy but on its validity as a first-hand view of African-American slavery."[42]

Bond might have questioned the virtues of publication not only because of its effect on texts but because of the experiences of fellow African American writers like Phillis Wheatley, Harriet Jacobs, and even Frederick Douglass. If literacy was a crime for African Americans, authorship was a lifelong sentence: Wheatley died in poverty; Wilson reinvented herself as a beautician and mystic; Douglass made abolition and civil rights his life's work, as did many other African Americans who sought publication as a means toward social justice. In contrast, Bond stayed away from the hubbub of the literary marketplace, where economics met reform and capital produced culture. To protect her project, she needed to preserve her privacy, as she does in the novel's closing narrative events, where, as noted earlier, Bond and Hannah relate neither Hannah's miraculous reunion with her long-lost and hitherto unknown mother nor her eventual choice to marry. In her own life, Bond never linked herself with any of the larger civil rights organizations or even with a larger public. Unlike Sojourner Truth, she did not choose self-publication as an option. Rather, to preserve her privacy and her freedom, she maintained her "silent unobtrusive way" while exercising her powers of expression. As a text that speaks to all sorts of oppression—sexual, racial, and class-based—Bond's novel achieves its intrinsic power in writing, not in publication.

Bond's commitment to her own literary freedom can be seen in one last bit of material evidence: her self-fashioned title page (fig. 8), which provides visual proof of the contingent and mutually constitutive relationship between book, author, and identity. The handwritten title emphasizes the singularity of the text, setting off the demonstrative adjective "The" on its own line. Bond appears as the generative nucleus at the center, visually and (so the book's publication will argue) historically holding together this package of literary history. Literally and figuratively using her hand to manufacture established literary trappings, Bond makes each line further elaborate the intricacies of text, author, and publication, conveying an expectation or fantasy that the manuscript will be seen, even as the very handwriting repudiates publication.

Hannah Bond's identity as an author might seem as virtual as her Wikipedia entry: both appear in the context of the positivist world of information gathering, and both are written in the conditional mood, suggesting a wished-for identity that has yet to be proved. As we have seen, Bond's text is mediated through a variety of literacies, including the protocols of fiction and literature. In apparently choosing to write fiction, she gave herself an extra measure of freedom from racially imposed generic standards, even as she probably knew her choice would negatively affect the book's market potential. Or, as I have been arguing, Bond intentionally eschewed the market in order to produce and then protect her aesthetic—and ultimately political—project.

Bond is not just an author, and *The Bondwoman's Narrative* is not just another novel. Both Bond and her novel play a revisionary role in literary and cultural history. From the early efforts of abolitionists to more recent debates over "firsts," the challenge of documenting (and evaluating) African American literary history has been a battleground for disputes over ideology, aesthetics, and everything in between. The liminal status of Bond's manuscript text points to the protocols that are equally necessary for the codex and the born-digital. Without the confirmation

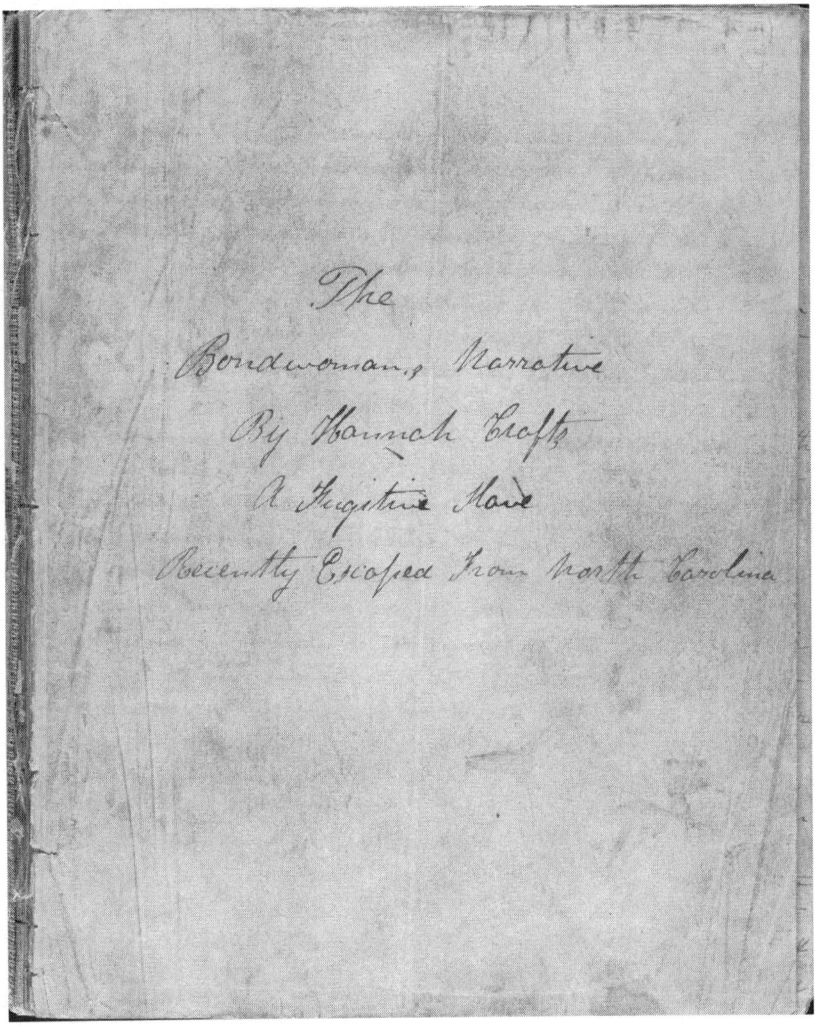

The
Bondwomans Narrative
By Hannah Crafts
A Fugitive Slave
Recently Escaped From North Carolina

Figure 8. Facsimile reproduction of the title page of the holographic manuscript of *The Bondwoman's Narrative* by Hannah Crafts. It reads: "The Bondwoman's Narrative / By Hannah Crafts / A Fugitive Slave / Recently Escaped From South Carolina."

process bestowed by Gates's scholarly apparatus, *The Bondwoman's Narrative* and its author would face the epistemic problems generated by the mashed-up proliferation of image, text, and idea in the Web 2.0 world. Bond needed the scholarly imprint provided by traditional publishing. Because the stakes of her success are so deeply enmeshed with cultural values and priorities, the kind of freedom afforded by unconventional routes of publication would not have benefited her. As with Wheatley before her, her place in history had to be secured through a confirmation process governed by experts. Perhaps Bond knew, however, that as Frances Smith Foster observes, "Wheatley's literary achievements may have facilitated her eventual freedom but . . . had not protected her finally from the ravages of racial discrimination and poverty." Foster concludes, "It took more than words to change society and . . . words would be subjected to interpretations engendered by non-literary expectations and assumptions."[43] In the nineteenth century, Bond and her manuscript had to remain unknown in order to be free. Thus the manuscript of *The Bondwoman's Narrative* holds the coveted position once accorded the book as a cultural signifier. Even now that it is bound between two covers, it forces us to think outside the book.

CHAPTER 4

Testimony (The Edition Reimagined)

The first edition, established and maintained as a scholarly benchmark, has slowly lost its position. Its slide began when literary scholars and bibliographers joined forces to create the "critical edition," which trumped the authorial imprint of the first edition with the added expertise of the professional critic and historian.[1] The field of textual criticism arose in response to this change, and most scholars would now agree with Jerome McGann that "there is no such thing as a 'bad text.'"[2] Today, following the example of William Charvart and his analysis of Longfellow, scholars treat editions as palimpsests, layered archives out of which emerge not just multiple texts but evidence of the efforts of authors, editors, and publishers to negotiate and intervene in literary markets as well as in the generic expectations that guide them.[3]

In this chapter I reexamine the edition as a functional scholarly myth in the wake of these movements in the field—and in anticipation of the scholarly issues that emerge as texts become increasingly affected by social media. Extending John Bryant's notion of the fluid text to include the contributions of readers and their annotations, I argue that editions are not merely as fluid as Bryant finds *Typee* but exponentially more so.[4] The 2.0 digital world has done more than simply make texts available.

Free e-texts such as those offered by Project Gutenberg paved the way for ever-changing electronic texts inflected by readers through Web 2.0 applications like SocialBook and other crowd-sourced annotations.[5] These new media awaken us to the idea that everything is a medium, transforming static concepts such as the edition into fluid notions about production, reception, and reproduction. As a result, the scholarly emphases on textual authenticity (the first edition) and textual authority (the critical edition) must now make way for the reader/writer whose interaction with the text promises to invigorate and transform literary studies. As Bob Stein predicts in the documentation for SocialBook, "electronic 'books' over time will evolve into an unimaginable variety of forms; the one constant will be the presumption of a social element."[6]

But is this social element really new? Older print forms may seem unrelated to born-digital literary objects, but in fact the two share more than scholars typically acknowledge. New media studies suggest that, rather than linking the book's modal stability with the epistemic features associated with print culture, we should think of editions along the lines of digital texts, for which the probability of propagating "endlessly and effortlessly" is definitional rather than exceptional or new.[7] My argument here hinges on the reader's role in this propagation: I debunk distinctions between the traditional codex and the "born-digital" by focusing on the palimpsestuous nature of text as perpetually inflected by readers. Interpretation is not just the purview of scholars but an ongoing and necessary activity built into language and human culture.[8] The attention brought to the effects of composition and reception by scholars of digital technology alerts us to how certain terms—such as "book" or "edition"—"encourage," as Michael Kirschenbaum writes, "too much detachment from the realities of the network environment in which the work is . . . irretrievably situated."[9] In previous chapters I suggested that relaxing the hard-and-fast distinctions between forms—oral, print, visual—does not threaten their (or our) authority, but rather assists us in understanding their complexity. This chapter breaks the cultural circuit of author, editor, and publisher delimited by the single edition to restore the importance of the nineteenth-century and contemporary reader alike in making meaning from texts, both material and digital.

My exploration of the malleability of editions centers on Augusta Jane Evans's 1864 novel *Macaria*, a book with an apocryphal past. *Macaria* invites women to follow the example of the mythic Macaria, who sacrificed herself for the good of her country. The book was considered a piece of Southern propaganda, but its publication history belies its status as a sectional novel, for it was published simultaneously on both sides of the Mason-Dixon line during the Civil War.[10] Although earlier critics, scholars, and biographers have treated *Macaria*'s appearance in the North as unauthorized, Melissa Homestead's painstakingly detailed publication history reveals that the novel was deliberately transported to New York to allow for a nearly simultaneous publication.[11] By dispensing with the romantic lie of the "bootleg" edition, Homestead shows that the distinction between Northern and Southern readerships was a scholarly invention rather than an accurate reflection of contemporary reading practices. The publication history of the novel thus complicates the scholarly preference for the first edition: neither and both of the Northern and Southern versions of *Macaria* are first editions, foregrounding the porous nature of the text. These almost simultaneous editions thus tell an important story about the interplay between author, text, edition, and reader—even as the novel itself remains virtually the same.[12]

N. Katherine Hayles argues that print and digital text are enhanced by and intertwined with each other. "They tend to morph into one another," she writes, "much as a Moebius surface goes from inside to outside to inside, so there is necessarily a certain amount of arbitrariness in labeling a given instance as either imitating electronic textuality or intensifying print traditions."[13] This recognition of the intertwining and continuous nature of text reflects the impact of new media, but it also foregrounds the human element that threads throughout Robert Darnton's model of the communication circuit, which identifies publication as a complex social network. From Hayles and Darnton, we learn that each element or stage in the process of publication offers multiple opportunities for interpretation (see fig. 1). Darnton's diagram shows how the route a text travels, as it navigates the serpentine progress from manuscript to publication to bookseller to reader, is speckled with a variety of interpolations. A book's size, cover, and typeface shape its reception, as do the locations in which it becomes available, from bookstall to library and reading club; at each publishing decision point, a text is routinely and purposefully put into and developed by interpretive contexts. The study of editions fits into this theoretical framework because editions represent, in their various iterations, not simply a mechanical process of reproduction, but transformations that are very much inflected by the social dynamics of the publication process. From cover art to chapter headings and illustrations, editions are immediate products of social environments, generated by larger cultural cycles. Subject to a multitude of forces, editions change over time and testify to the reading cultures out of which they emerge.

Editions thus can be seen as physical manifestations of specific aesthetic values—values through which the reader, as much as the author, stakes a claim in the cultural marketplace. Borrowing from Clifford Geertz, the cultural anthropologist and author of the groundbreaking article "Deep Play," we might see in the proliferation of editions what he saw in the Balinese cockfight: "a metasocial commentary upon the whole matter of assorting human beings into fixed hierarchical ranks and then organizing the major part of collective existence around that assortment. Its function, if you want to call it that, is interpretive: it is a Balinese reading of Balinese experience; a story they tell themselves about themselves."[14] Likewise, we can treat not just the emergence of an edition but the successive reemergence of new editions as part of a collective testimony in which authors, editors, publishers, and readers combine to tell a collective story.

After its initial appearance in 1864, *Macaria* went through at least six subsequent editions and reprintings over a thirty-year period.[15] Its popularity on both sides of the Mason-Dixon line, before and after the war, indicates that it was not simply a sectional novel. Rather, the novel traversed regional and historical distinctions: it emerged during the Civil War and continued to find a readership through the fall of the South, the failure of Reconstruction, and the rise of the New South. Evans, who was said to have sold almost half a million copies of her novels, thus takes her place among the super-producers Hawthorne railed against.[16] She reputedly garnered "15,000 dollars for a manuscript sight unseen."[17] According to Elizabeth Moss, Evans was highly invested in her professional success: she was more concerned about her ability to sell her work than with her legitimacy as a writer, "indicating a great degree of awareness about the profession."[18]

It might seem that Evans's success as an author would bar her from a study that challenges the primacy of the book as a signifier of literary culture and cultural value. The peculiar publication history of *Macaria*, however, with its mix of personal, aesthetic, regional, and political concerns, complicates the book's status as a relatively stable single-authored text. Evans did not significantly revise *Macaria* over time or according to particular circumstances of publication. Aside from shearing off her 1864 dedication to the Confederate soldiers, she left the text relatively unchanged across its editions. In contrast to the case of Melville and *Typee*, reprinted editions of *Macaria* thus gauge the tastes of readers more than they register authorial intervention and interpolation.[19] In light of Franco Moretti's suggestion that we factor together the massive production of novels with the exceptional cases on which we base literary histories, the novel's multiple editions over time and region make it an important example for this study. Encouraging literary critics and historians to use a different form of conceptual organization in categorizing literary work—the many instead of the one, the collectivity rather than the exception—Moretti notes that "abstraction is not an end in itself, but a way to widen the domain of the literary historian, and enrich its internal problematic."[20] In this chapter, three strands of analysis—of Evans's history, the history of her novel, and the novel itself—braid together theoretical questions about the intertwining of author and edition, reader and text.

From Minervy to Minerva: Regional to Radical

Augusta Jane Evans was born in Georgia in 1835. After a brief stint in Texas, her family settled in Mobile, Alabama, where they soon experienced a reversal of fortune. Evans had no formal education. According to her biographer William Perry Fidler, her 1854 novel *Inez* was penned in secret as a Christmas present to her father and appeared in print a year later.[21] Evans published this first work with Harper's, though her biographer guesses that "this established firm probably received a subsidy large enough to cover the costs of one edition" from a member of her extended family. Despite the book's contested financing, the fact that she chose to publish in New York indicates an early understanding of the literary marketplace and its workings.[22]

One aspect of the book's genesis, however, sets the novel outside the familiar narrative of professional authorship, especially for women, which has come to dominate the literary history of the nineteenth century.

Although the fifteen-year-old Evans feared that her parents wouldn't approve of her writing, she had ruled out other means of making a living, a necessary preoccupation given the loss of the family fortune in the 1840s. She knew that teaching would be an acceptable job, but she did not have the requisite educational background. Those familiar with nineteenth-century American literature might recognize the similarity of this story to the history and plot of *Little Women.* Like Louisa May Alcott and her literary creation Jo March, Evans turned to writing as a means to support her family. But unlike that of the Northern women writers with whom she might be compared, Evans's early success depended on her adoring, supportive, and self-sacrificing slave.

Evans credited the existence of *Inez* to the help of a slave named Minervy. She cast this female house slave, whose name is a colloquial version of "Minerva," the Roman goddess of wisdom, in a picturesque role as a young writer's sole support. The story of Minervy's help was handed down by Evans herself through her best friend, Rachel Lyons. According to Lyons, Minervy provided Evans with oil for her lamp to write at night, helping her keep her scribbling a secret by day while making sure that her writing did not undermine her health.[23]

This story calls for more analysis than it has been given, especially as Evans deliberately propagated it, linking her early success as an author to the Southern model of slavery. Read metaphorically, slavery provides sustenance for Evans's creative and physical well-being. But Evans's intentional inclusion of Minervy in her own history also highlights just how important slavery was to crafting her identity as an author. The story was recirculated in Evans's obituary, which quoted the letter from Lyons, solidifying its place in her authorial legacy. This third-hand slavery-based history provides further context for the apocryphal story of *Macaria* as a contraband text smuggled across enemy lines and published without the author's knowledge in the North. The story of Minervy, whether true or false, not only establishes how Evans became an author but also embellishes her status as a Southern author.[24]

The plot and publication history of *Beulah*, Evans's next novel, offer evidence of her growing sophistication as a writer and promoter of her work. Over the span of more than five hundred pages, the novel's title character comes to understand the power of womanly intuition. Like *Macaria*'s Irene, Beulah teaches readers that womanly virtue is mystically endowed with womanly intuition. It is a source of guidance for her and those she loves, as well as a means to obtain a place in heaven. By the end of the novel, Beulah has reconciled her faith and converted the soul of her mate, assuring a place in heaven for both of them.[25]

Evans's efforts to bring *Beulah* to print reflect her increasing confidence in her career as a novelist. She first sent the manuscript to Daniel Appleton, who rejected it as soon as she arrived in New York with her cousin Colonel John W. Jones.[26] Evans promptly contacted J. C. Derby of the publishers Derby & Jackson, a well-informed choice. Derby & Jackson had brought other female Southern novelists into print, including Mary Virginia Terhune, who wrote under the nom de plume "Marion Harland" and in 1852 published one of the anti–*Uncle Tom's Cabin* novels then popular in the South.[27] Derby agreed to take the novel if his family liked it; *Beulah* would succeed—or fail—according to the domesticated tastes of home and hearth. This "shrewd decision," according to Fidler, "illustrates Derby's awareness of the tastes to which the novel was addressed." It also mirrors a review process used by the Boston publisher James T. Fields, as well as Nathaniel Hawthorne and Mark Twain, all of whom deferred to the opinions of the female readers in their households. The Derby women's positive assessment of the manuscript accurately predicted its subsequent success. The Evans family used the profits from *Beulah* to purchase a house.[28]

With Evans's success as a novelist secured, she turned her attention away from Miner*vy* to Miner*va*, the virgin goddess of warriors, poetry, medicine, wisdom, and commerce, and the inventor of music.[29] In a series of critical pieces published in the *Mobile Daily Advertiser* during the fall of 1859, between the publication of *Beulah* and *Macaria*, Evans enlightened readers as to the purpose of literature and explained why Southern writers had not yet succeeded in meeting the high standards she described. The articles indicate Evans's sense of her place in the publishing market and her conviction that she and all Southern writers must intervene in the development of the literary marketplace. In attacking that bastion of Northern superiority, literary culture, she argued that the publishing centers of Philadelphia, Boston, and New York were able to promote and dominate what the world understood as "American" literature through business acumen rather than the appreciation of literary merit. She thus anticipated an argument that would not be fully fleshed out until the late twentieth century, when William Charvat ushered in the critical study of the publishing industry that today's scholars take for granted.[30]

Evans's strategy was to release "Literature" (with a capital L) from the mundane concerns of contemporary culture.[31] Charging that Northern authors were pandering to politics as a way to make a living through their writing, Evans most consistently attacks the humanitarian realism born of the abolitionist movement. She urges her friend Rachel Lyons to "select only the very highest types of character" to write about, "for the standard has sadly deteriorated of late in works of fiction. In a too close imitation of Nature, many of our novelists have fallen into the error of patronizing coarseness, vulgarity, and ignorance."[32] In her advice to another friend and would-be novelist, Evans, perhaps combining scorn for her competition with critical evaluation of the reigning literary standards, points to George Eliot's 1859 novel *Adam Bede*, with its explicit social agenda expressed through its focus on lower-class characters and sensationalist plotlines, as a prime example of the collapsing standards of taste.

In addition to criticizing the tendency of Northern authors to privilege historically specific realist aesthetics, Evans also attacks the formal conventions of their publications themselves, charging that "the *bloated* size of most of their sheets enables them to spread before the reader writing that would do honor to any age, in loathsome proximity to that which is too vulgar for street reading, and yet, side by side the wise Minerva and grim Cerberus enter into the sacred presence of our Household Gods, and the monster does not blush to go there. Nay, in too many instances, his presence is welcomed whilst his fair companion is turned from the door."[33] Evans decries the hodgepodge of magazines and broadsheets that emphasize quantity over quality, likening the contemporary literary output she disdains to the flesh-eating three-headed dog that stands guard at the gates of Hades. Fidler characterizes her strategy as "shrewd propaganda, no matter what one may think of its historical and critical accuracy," even venturing that "perhaps she had learned good lessons from the clever propagandists of Abolition—Mrs. Stowe, Garrison, Whittier, even Lincoln."[34] The lessons may have included excising her own history of an earlier Minerva: the slave woman Minervy who helped her pen *Inez*. By contrast, this Minerva, fair and rejected, hovers helplessly outside the household's door.

Postulating a Kantian theory of beauty in her articles, Evans insists that authors must write not for the contemporary reader but rather for all time, focusing on "the elaboration of topics which should immortalize both the writer and the subject matter of his discourse." She believes that the trouble with much of the work of Southern—and Northern—writers is that their writing fails to resonate deeply, that is, to address concerns that exceed both their region and their time. (That her own work continued to appeal and speak to readers across region, time, and political affiliations suggests that she more than realized her ideals.) The focus on regional concerns and sectional differences has, in turn, downgraded critical gatekeeping. She observes, "There is a rapidly growing tendency among Southern writers of the present day to extol with indiscriminate praise whatever proceeds from a Southern pen, and to berate, with unbecoming severity, whatever originates on the other side of 'Mason and Dixon's Line.'"[35] Echoing the historically more prominent writer of the South, Edgar Allan Poe, Evans makes it clear that both writers and critics, two powerful vehicles of cultural production, are equally responsible for the lack of worthwhile literature.

Evans's concerns also indicate the historical value she places on literary production: like the hieroglyphs of ancient Egypt, novels will remain the culture's testament to its past. Evans is most interested in the novel (over the years she published nine) for its ability, in Geertz's words, "to entangle [in-wrought] perceptions" of the reader "somehow with the equally in-wrought perceptions of the people" she is trying to represent *and* inspire: her readers.[36] The publication and reception of *Macaria* can be seen as proof of her vision. The novel circulated widely and found its way into a camp of Union troops; it was subsequently burned and banned by their commander for its sympathetic treatment of Southern characters.[37] Yet *Macaria*'s success—emphasized by its incendiary reception—testifies to tastes driven as much by the generic expectations of readers as by ideological viewpoint. Union leaders claimed that they banned the book because the characters in *Macaria* were so sympathetically drawn; in Evans's terms, they were, perhaps, "the very highest types of characters," rather than coarse regional stereotypes, so that even their purported enemies could engage with them. Indeed, if Harriet Beecher Stowe is known as the woman who started the war, we might see Evans as the woman who threatened, if not to stop it, to change its terms radically.[38]

Macaria: How the Lost Cause Kept Its Voice

Macaria is frequently likened to *Uncle Tom's Cabin,* for it galvanized readers on both sides of the Mason-Dixon line to take action through its sympathetic treatment of the South and the Southern war effort. Yet readers today may be surprised to find the novel's treatment of slavery scant and its discussion of Confederate politics even scanter. Instead, *Macaria* focuses on the multiple sacrifices made by its main character, Irene Huntingdon, and her companions in order to uphold and further uplift Southern culture. Indeed, some twenty-seven chapters pass before the reader encounters any direct argument for the South or the Confederacy, which, when it does appear, takes place on constitutional grounds, specifically around the issue of habeas corpus. In emphasizing the rule of law rather than sectional ideology, Evans follows a strategy adopted by other secessionists while also keeping her story true to the poetics she espoused in her critical writing.

If the South is one of the novel's preoccupations, gender is another. Though a staunch supporter of the Confederacy in all its iterations, in *Macaria* Evans negotiates a complex critique of Southern white women, for whom slavery had created, in her opinion, an unhealthy leisure, disassociating them from an invigorating sense of "duty." The novel's solution is not, however, the abolition of slavery but rather the reinvention of a model of womanly duty outside marriage.[39] Part of *Macaria*'s appeal, then, was to female readers who were wondering how to fulfill their sense of civic duty. As the popularity of the novel on both sides of the Mason-Dixon line attests, this focus had much to offer readers at home while most marriageable men were either away in battle or soon to join the warring forces.

In terms of those battles and warring forces, *Macaria* was the product of much firsthand research. Conversant with many of the higher-ups in the Confederacy—General P. G. T. Beauregard sent her a diamond-studded pen in recognition of her wartime service as a propagandist and nurse—Evans studs her novel with fact.[40] Making fact a principal part of her story's moral and spiritual legitimacy was her contribution to the war effort.[41] Of the novel supposedly "scribbled in pencil" while Evans was "sitting up with sick soldiers in the hospital attached to 'Camp Beulah,'" she confided, "My very heart beats in its pages, coarse and brown though the dear old Confederate paper was."[42] Evans's attachment to the idea of female sacrifice for the war effort also had personal roots. Before the war, she had fallen in love with James Reed Spaulding, a New York editor and journalist. They had planned a trip to meet her parents in Mobile, but the war intervened. She later broke off the engagement because of their sectional differences; he went on to write editorials for the *New York Times* in support of Lincoln.[43] If *Macaria* does not recount this experience, it surely draws upon its emotional resonances.

Although the broad popularity of the novel attests to its successful temporizing, critics have not appreciated how Evans's emphasis on the common soldier, as opposed to the aristocratic leaders of the Confederacy, contributed to its lasting success. *Macaria*'s focus on the common man aligns with much of the war writing of the period, from Louisa May Alcott to Walt Whitman. Although she was Beauregard's adviser and confidante, Evans downplayed his importance in her depictions of battles. Rather, as Alice Fahs points out, Evans's omniscient third-person narrator valorizes the common soldier by bringing the reader to his bedside and remarking, "We are indebted for freedom to the uncomplaining fortitude and sublime devotion of the private soldiers of the Confederacy, not less than to the genius of our generals and the heroism of our subordinate officers." Placing the "private soldiers" alongside the "generals" and "officers" frames democracy as a Confederate principle.[44]

Evans's notion of what Geertz calls "deep play" is at the heart of both her project to improve American literature and her success as a novelist. Interpreting the historical reception of *Macaria* demands that we inflect the homology of its readers across regional lines—both North and South—an adaptation that *Uncle Tom's Cabin* does not require of us. The response to *Uncle Tom's Cabin* was as overdetermined as its message. Some loved and others abhorred it, but all agreed that its driving principle was to abolish slavery. The novel's spin-offs and parodies—from plays, sheet music, dolls, and toys to anti-*Tom* literature—suggest how deeply the culture resonated with its message, whether for or against it.[45] The reception history of *Macaria*, however, resists the easy distinctions between North and South by temporalizing and keeping Evans's portrayal of women away from the "patronizing coarseness, vulgarity, and ignorance" she abhorred in the popular fiction of the period according to her model of literary merit. Indeed, *Macaria*'s success with readers validates Evans's sense that they wanted less realism and more idealism.

The dedication to the novel's first Confederate edition declares Evans's allegiance to the common soldier. Regretting that she is unable to fight, she nonetheless expresses her admiration for "the deathless glory of the 'tented field.'" The novel's cover (fig. 9), by contrast, articulates an understanding of Evans's relationship to her readers: "BY THE AUTHOR OF 'BEULAH.'" These words appear in capital letters in the same smaller font used for the "OR" in the title, *Macaria; or, Altars of Sacrifice.* The choice of font and size visually reinforces the sense of authorship as opening up and allowing a series of alternate identities; it thus echoes the contrast in the way Evans conceives of herself at once as someone excluded from the battlefield and as the author of *Beulah*, that is, in personal and political terms on the one hand and in professional and commercial terms on the other. The dedication and cover thus stitch together a series of relationships—woman, soldier, author, novel—that inform Evans's views on literature and her use of publishing signifiers as a tool for understanding its power.

A prominent advertisement in the *Mobile Daily Advertiser and Register*, made even more noticeable by its placement within a box, embroiders still another likeness for Evans. Here she is dubbed "the Madame De Stael of the South," and her book is "The great Romance." The copy boldly claims *Macaria*'s virtues: it is "a romance of eminent intellectual power, as far above the contemporary English Novel as *Les Misérables* is above all Novels. It is a Southern Book, relating the woeful incidents of the time, but without a rival in interest and artistic beauty."[46] Having it both ways, as it were—or perhaps every which way—the advertisement situates the novel within the category of works that focus on the human condition, like *Les Misérables*, and recommends it to Southern readers who feel victimized and oppressed by the politically powerful North, while still hailing its artistry.[47]

We find evidence of Evans's deliberate and canny choices to manifest her literary views in the opening chapters of the novel. Although the novel is titled *Macaria*, preparing readers for a female protagonist, Evans begins not with a woman but with the image of a town clock striking midnight and a candle burning down. The words "flickering light fell on grim battalions of figures" suggests a war novel, but the "figures" actually refer

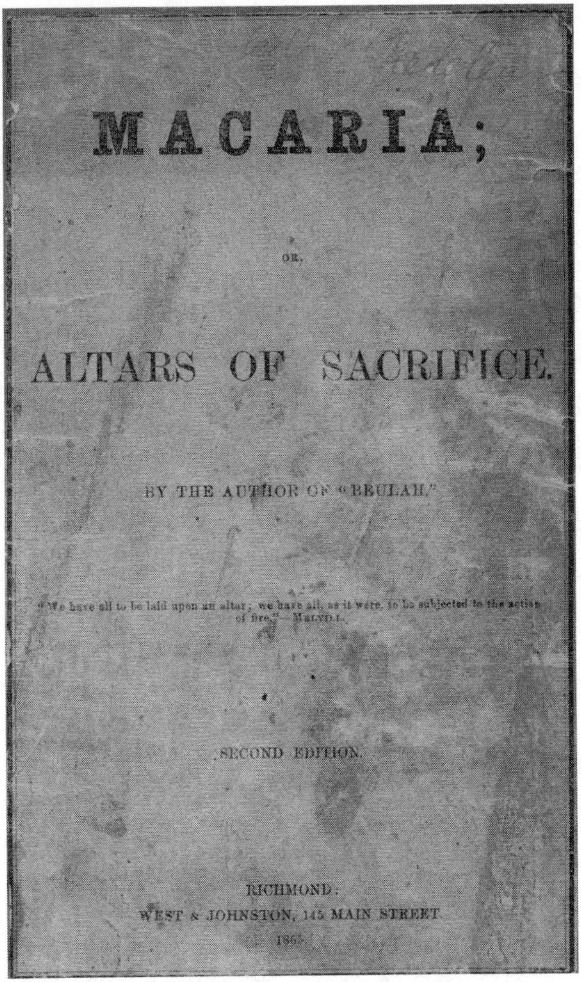

Figure 9. Front cover of *Macaria* by Augusta Jane Evans. Image courtesy of Documenting the American South, The University of North Carolina at Chapel Hill Libraries.

not to soldiers but to numbers in a ledger that an accountant struggles to reconcile late into the night. This first character we meet is a strapping young man, Russell Aubrey, who immediately registers as exceptional, for "in these later days of physical degeneration, such athletic frames as his are rarely seen among the youth of our land," and he seems to be able to maintain this physical excellence in spite of the demands placed on him by his job and, we later learn, his history.[48] The description of

Aubrey's physique evokes the ancient Spartan aesthetic and thus focuses the novel's critical energies on rejuvenating society (and culture) through the collective strength of individuals.

One of this central character's prevailing struggles is his legacy. "I am Russell Aubrey," he announces, "the despised son of a ——" (6). Using the mask of decorum, Evans provocatively leaves it up to the reader to decide just what his shameful past might be. We meet Aubrey as he intends to "rake up the smoldering ashes of a miserable Past to fling in the face and blind me. . . . I will gather up these same ashes, dry and bitter, and hide them with sacred zeal in a golden urn" (6). Reaching for the upper case in order to imbue his sense of history with mythological status, Evans enacts her own edict that literature refrain from temporizing and instead focus on eternal values. As a result, Aubrey's story is not limited to a particular moment in time. As the novel's persistent popularity demonstrates, his resilience comes to stand as effectively for the vanquished South as for the fighting South. Readers learn toward the end of the first chapter that Aubrey's father was a suicide, which makes Aubrey's story represent Southern tenacity. At this point Evans introduces Irene, the novel's main character, who is willing to invest and sacrifice in order to save the South. Although the novel focuses on her story, it has already been set up as the story of a valiant culture and its struggle to survive through the efforts of its (female) members.

Utilizing stereotypes to evoke sympathy with the same masterly touch as Charles Dickens, Evans presents the narrative arc of her characters' actions, lives, and choices in a manner that reinforces the novel's claim to satisfy the eternal principles of beauty. Readers of *Macaria* encounter an aging mother, a deserving (and beautiful) orphan, and an unorthodox but surprisingly ethical lawyer. The story reinforces the "eternal" values of family through its depictions of these characters and the circumstances in which they find themselves. Not simply powerful metaphors for the South, these archetypes teach readers that they must live beyond history. Their pasts, like Aubrey's, have had serious repercussions on their futures and the futures of those they encounter. All of this, as the novel's subtitle, *Altars of Sacrifice*, suggests, will require losses in the interest of the future.

Evans reaches for the upper case on the subject of "Law" just as she does on the subject of literature. The narrative emphasis on the inviolacy of the rule of law to the Southern nation, which echoes the argument made throughout the Confederacy concerning Lincoln's suspension of habeas corpus, is explored through the sentimental plot strand concerning Russell Aubrey's past and subsequent relationship with the most fair-minded and sympathetic of characters, the lawyer Campbell. It is to Mr. Campbell that the wealthy plantation heiress Irene turns when she wants to alleviate the financial difficulty facing the Aubrey household, so that her friend Electra can continue her studies, and it is Mr. Campbell who sees through the accusation that Russell is a thief and subsequently hires him as an assistant and apprentice. Through Mr. Campbell, Law not only prevails but ensures a just outcome as well for even the most misunderstood characters. Remaining focused on the rule of law and constitutional rights allows the novel to escape being pigeonholed by its sectional politics.

Evans's penetration of the literary marketplace by placing two editions of the novel in multiple venues reflects her knowledge of the politicization of reading and readership. If we recall her articles in the *Mobile Daily Advertiser*, we can see how *Macaria* accomplished what she describes as literature's cultural work. Evans objected to the use of literature for political purposes because of its debasing effect, and she took issue with the temporizing effects of realism, especially in the hands of Northern writers. She believed instead that literature ought to be limited to "the elaboration of topics which should immortalize both the writer and the subject matter of his discourse."[49] Thus, though she clearly operated with a canny understanding of the political implications of her writing, she focused not on immediate social change but rather on the power of literature to "lift" and restore culture. Novels, especially those that reappear in multiple editions, are a testament to a culture's enduring values. We see precisely how Evans imagined these values in the way *Macaria* exalts traditions, affirming the value of the past and of long-lived cultural meaning rather than immediate political imperatives.

Readers then and now may very well be overwhelmed by the proliferation of Greek and Latin names, places, and references, but Evans has a clear purpose. When she writes, for instance, that Irene "with fond, womanly pride . . . was wont to recur to her lonely observatory in Silesia, where, before Newton rose upon the world, one of her own sex, Maria Cunitz, launched upon the stormy sea of scientific literature the 'Urania Propitia'" (177), she posits her character as a model for her readers, who are also meant to "recur" with "fond pride" to the power and glory of the name-rich past. Called a "remembrancer" by one critic, Evans used erudite references to evoke a better time, or as William Fidler puts it, as "cherished reminders of social traditions and standards of conduct once honored but often forgotten in a later day."[50] Anticipating T. S. Eliot's 1922 masterwork *The Waste Land*, Evans confers cultural legitimacy through cultural literacy. Like Eliot's poem, *Macaria* would benefit from a set of footnotes—or lend itself to an Internet-enabled publication format such as hypertext.[51] But Evans intends readers who fail (or don't bother) to understand her allusions to be lost, just as Eliot did (before Pound intervened); her own lack of formal education makes these markers of education, themselves signifiers of a transcendent classical culture, all the more precious.

The character Irene, who is, among other things, a model for female agency Southern-style, is one of the reasons why *Macaria* was so successful, both during and after the war, and her roots, too, lie in classical models. In a letter to her close friend Lyons, Evans extolled Irene, declaring her "the noblest character I ever painted" and the "ideal of perfect womanhood."[52] Critics have struggled to come to terms with the meaning of "perfect womanhood"; the self-sacrificing Irene seems very much at odds with key aspects of the narrative, namely, Evans's formal challenges to the Southern domestic tradition as represented by Caroline Hentz, author of the popular rebuttal to *Uncle Tom's Cabin*, *The Planter's Northern Bride* (1854), among other books.[53] One way to explain Evans's representation of Irene is through the centrality of sacrifice to the novel's plot. According to Drew Gilpin Faust, "Evans intended the novel both as her own contribution to Confederate nationalism and as a narrative that would provide women with models for emulation in their search for 'agency' within the Confederate cause" (xvii). Sacrifice is key to the development of Irene's agency—and key to the novel's popularity on both sides of the Mason-Dixon line, both during and after the Civil War.

Evans underscores the importance of sacrifice in the novel's title. In Greek mythology, Macaria is known for her willingness to sacrifice herself for the good of the state, in strong contrast to Antigone, who defies the king in order to honor her brother's burial rites. Macaria, the daughter of Heracles, appears in Euripides' play *Heraclidae* (The Children of Heracles). The play describes her noble sacrifice: to die for her siblings and save Athens. The spring where she died is named the Macarian spring in her honor.[54]

Macaria's heroine Irene—named after the Greek goddess who signifies peace—is the character who embodies the values evoked by the title. Irene represents the frustration of women excluded from the war because of gender; her struggles throughout the novel reflect the fierce determination to contribute nonetheless. Irene explains her rationale for breaking the conventions for female behavior in marital terms. "Mothers and wives are, in most instances, kept at home," she observes, but she, like the virgin goddess Minerva, has "nothing to bind her," so she may take up the "sacred duty" of nursing soldiers, for single women have "the privilege of carrying light and blessings to many firesides—of being the friend and helper of hundreds," whereas married women contribute to the happiness and comfort of just one hearth. In this context, the invaluable role of the unmarried woman is simply to take the functions of wife and mother and apply them to the wider world, not just the home. Argued forcefully in both plot and generic structure, this viewpoint suggests that the existing norms need only be extended, not revised.[55]

One way Evans connects with a broad readership is by empowering her female figures, and one of Irene's crucial avenues to power is science, which is in turn another important way that Evans reached mid-nineteenth-century readers on both sides of the Mason-Dixon line. As Irene is an astronomer, her interest in science is central to how she spends her time, but it also underwrites her tendency to analyze circumstances and events objectively; that is, it justifies what might seem like male thinking in a female character. Like *Macaria*'s classical allusions and references, astronomy also moves the novel beyond the limits of region. A science linked by the stars rather than national boundaries, astronomy offers an entrée to the international community the South wishes to join.[56]

Yet despite the popularity of astronomy at the time, Irene is the only female astronomer in a novel by a nineteenth-century American women writer, from the North or South.[57] Nina Baym notes that although Evans takes great care to develop the idea of the female scientist, in the end, Irene's devotion to astronomy is more "a form of private worship" than the inauguration of a new professional choice for women (165–66). But if as a sociological tool *Macaria* fails to provide a prototype for a professional woman scientist, as a literary device, Irene's character supports Evans's critique of white upper-class Southern womanhood, whose extinction in its present fetishized and overspecialized form is inevitable. In this light, the fizzling of Irene's future as a scientist is less a failure of imagination than a powerful instrument in the service of Evans's larger argument.[58]

Although Irene may not have a future as a scientist, Evans takes pains to connect her to important female forebears and thus to situate her in history. The sixteenth-century astronomer Maria Cunitz, who revised Kepler's tables with a view toward their practical application, serves prominently not just as an influence but as an explicit model.[59] Although Evans could not have expected her readers to be familiar with all the figures she mentions, she took pains to make the allusions accurate and apropos. Given her general preference for Greek references, Evans could have modeled Irene on the Greek astronomer, mathematician, and philosopher Hypatia. But Hypatia's tragic end would not fit the narrative task at hand, given how purposefully the novel's deliberate—and selective—use of history yokes its analogies to Evans's arguments about both Southern culture and human culture.[60]

Maria Cunitz's interest in mathematics and astronomy was supported first by her father and later by her husband, Dr. Elias von Löwen, who publicly expressed his support by writing a preface to her book. By contrast, Irene's interest in science is more indulged than supported. Her father outfits the house with an observatory, complete with a telescope and an extensive library, but he takes issue with the importance and propriety of her studies. He finds her late nights unseemly, and he objects vehemently to "her devoting so large a share of her time and attention to this study, and has positively interdicted all observations after twelve o'clock" (176). Though she frequently disregards this restriction, she does so without making readers anxious about her conduct: her nocturnal activities do not take her out of the house.

The historical and practical facts of the profession of astronomy lend Irene both seriousness of mind and a certain panache. She is never seen in a dusty lab coat but wears long, flowing robes of sable-trimmed velvet that give her an irresistible aura of romance. If Irene were a chemist, Evans could make fertile kitchen metaphors, but she chooses instead to showcase her heroine's statuesque beauty as she leaves the drawing room to be viewed in the observatory by the third-person omniscient narrator—and the reader. Like the object of her study, she is as beautiful as she is remote and untouchable. Even though we are treated to a vision of her "in a loose wrapper, or robe de chambre, of black velvet, lined with crimson silk and girded with a heavy cord and tassel" out of which her "dimpled elbows" peek (173), the idea of touching her is as remote and far-fetched as touching the moon.

Astronomy also puts into perspective Irene's sacrifice of romantic love to duty, for it reveals earthly existence to be just a speck on the cosmic plane. This larger perspective dwarfs even the solar system itself. As Irene puts it: "What mattered human labors, what need of trophies of human genius, of national grandeur, or individual glory? Eighteen million of years would level all in one huge, common, shapeless ruin. In comparison with the mighty mechanism of the astral system, the solar seemed a mere tiny cluster of jewels set in some infinite abyss; the sun shrank into insignificance, the moon waned, the planets became little gleaming points of light, such as her diamond ring threw off when held under gas-chandeliers" (178). Like human culture and the very solar system, so too the reader becomes aware of how small she is in the scheme of things. Astronomy becomes a tool for reinforcing the timeless ahistoricity Evans wants to evoke. By depersonalizing and, literally, un-grounding human experience, astronomy posits a refusal to dwell on the gritty consequences of war.

Finally, astronomy provides a plausible metaphorical substitute for romance. By the close of the novel, Irene finds her place not in the arms of her lover, as his wife and the mother of his children, but as a figurative wife and mother of the universe, modeling herself on the virgin goddess Minerva, a mythological figure who is represented in the stars. She explains:

> The head of a household, a wife and mother, is occupied with family cares and affections—can find little time for considering the comfort, or contributing to the enjoyment of any beyond the home-circle. Doubtless she is happier, far happier, than the unmarried woman; but to the last belongs the privilege of carrying light and blessings to many firesides—of being the friend and helper of hundreds; and because she belongs exclusively to no one, her heart expands to all her suffering fellow-creatures. . . . Remember that the

> woman who dares to live alone, and be sneered at, is braver, and nobler, and better than she who escapes both in a loveless marriage. (413–14)

To a war-ravaged woman of the North or South, these lines point the way to a redefinition of social purpose for women that does not include marriage. But if Irene is modeled on the Greek goddess Minerva, she also finds a source in Evans's childhood slave Minervy, who carried the light that enabled her to write her first novel. Subsuming Minervy into Minerva, Evans expresses a collective and collecting set of ideas that have complex roots in the *mentalité* of the time out of which they emerge.

Just as Evans purposefully deploys her sources, so she uses genre in ways that espouse a more radical message. Even as she maintains a degree of subservience to conventional moral and social codes regarding women, she formally eschews those conventions by putting politics at the center of the plot. Other key generic violations anticipate a modern, postbellum culture. The hero of the novel, Russell Aubrey, ends up dead, and the competing loves of his life, his orphaned cousin Electra and Irene, Electra's friend, are united through their devotion to him. They both remain unmarried, choosing to dedicate their lives to the good of others. The novel ends with this new social formation, diminished by war as the states have been, but persevering through the shared ideology of sacrifice.

In the book's final pages, we are left with the orphan artist Electra at her easel, painting her "Modern Macaria," modeled on her savior, Irene. Electra declares: "I want to lay my 'Modern Macaria,' as the first offering of Southern Art, upon my country's altar, as a nucleus around which nobler and grander pictures, from the hands of my countrymen and women, shall cluster" (409). She also articulates larger goals for a developing South: "In sunny climes like ours, my glorious Art had its birth, its novitiate, its apotheosis; and who dare say that future ages shall not find Art-students from all ages pressing, like pilgrims, to the Perfected School of the Southern States? Ancient republics offered premiums, and saw the acme of the arts; why not our Confederate republic, when days of national prosperity dawn upon us?" (409). Rather than posit a Confederate military triumph—the war was still raging when *Macaria* was first published—the novel explores a Southern future apart from politics.

In a brilliant move that helps explain the book's many reprintings over time, the novel does not present the North and South as opposed; instead it celebrates the differences between North and South, anticipating the reconciliation logic that permeated postbellum treatments of the conflict and made room for the South and its supporters to retain a sense of lost cause superiority. The two heroines call "the Southern planter class" to action, demanding that it live up to its purportedly noble resources. Irene describes what is needed to make this legacy reality. "In order to effect this 'consummation devoutly to be wished,'" she says, regarding her revolutionary plan to open a school for women, "it is necessary that the primary branches of Art should be popularized, and thrown open to the masses" (410).

Turning her attention to the philosophical tenets undergirding her theory, she calls on John Stuart Mill: "Mill contends, in his Political Economy, that the remuneration of the peculiar employments of women is always far below that of employments carried on by men, and he finds an explanation in the fact that they are overstocked. Hence in improving the condition of women, it is advisable to give them the readiest access to independent industrial pursuits, and extend the circle of their appropriate occupations" (410). Women, in the future state Irene imagines, will be compensated on the scale of their accomplishments, not according to the inequities dictated by gender norms. The outcome, however, will be achieved by maintaining the ideology of separate spheres.

Just as she risks alarming readers sensitive to changes in women's roles, Evans turns to history to settle their concerns: "Our Revolution has beggared thousands, and deprived many of their natural providers; numbers of women in the Confederacy will be thrown entirely upon their resources for maintenance. All can not be mantua-makers, milliners, or school-teachers; and in order to open up new avenues of support, I have determined so [*sic*] establish . . . a School of Design for women" (410). By leaving "our Revolution" without any further modification, Evans evokes the political history of early America as much as the battles of the time, commanding the power of history without its dulling limitations.

The key figure in this literary use of history is the reader, and the text's deliberate use of the privilege granted to the literary operates in the space between the time of writing and the time of reading. Part of Evans's genius rests in her ability to mobilize the language and concepts of democracy and freedom—words generated for a particular historical purpose—to support her Southern nationalism. Phrases taken from a variety of foundational documents, including the Declaration of Independence, speckle the speeches that Irene and others deliver throughout the novel. These references made it unnecessary for Evans to delete references to the Confederacy or the Southern planter class from later editions; instead, she could rely on the reader to discriminate between the novel's multiple layers of history, which stand in a palimpsestuous relationship to the text, seeping into it, leaving its tinge, without becoming it. In other words, the novel is presented as "deep play," its readers inflecting the story with contemporary meaning according to their time and historical circumstances. Shorn of its original front matter, the dedication to the soldiers of the Confederacy, and some of its more explicit pro-Southern sentiments, but otherwise largely stable, subsequent editions remained popular among a broad variety of readers.[61]

History, Testimony, and Editions

Slavery and sentiment are inextricably woven together in Evans's life and work, as we saw in her story about Minervy. Elizabeth Fekete Trubey notes that slavery and sentiment form "a complicated mire of affection and ownership, autonomy and obedience, submission and rebellion. Sentimental discourse in the South must be read in terms of how its writers both succeed and dramatically fail to negotiate between a vision of femininity and a position on slavery's legacy, between the languages of freedom and those of servitude, within the context of the Confederacy."[62] *Macaria*'s veritable silence on slavery might be construed as the kind of failure Trubey describes. Yet Evans's success as a novelist during and after the Civil War demonstrates the capaciousness of the literary and its ability to shape the way people think about themselves and others, fashioning their self-fashionings.[63] Perhaps even more powerfully, the popularity of *Macaria* over the years indicates not failure as Trubey suggests but the novel's elasticity.

Evans's third novel, *St. Elmo*, sold over a million copies within four months of its publication in 1866, making it the third-most-popular novel in nineteenth-century America.[64] After this astounding success, Evans turned her attention to writing what she called her "secret history of the

Confederacy,"[65] continuing to collect firsthand information from Confederate soldiers and officers as part of her plan to publish a documentary history of the war. She scuttled the project, however, out of respect for the former vice president of the Confederacy, Alexander Stephens, when she learned that he wanted to write his own history of the Confederacy. With deference to Stephens as both a man and a soldier, Evans wrote: "I humbly put the fingers on the throat of my ambitious daring design of becoming the Confederate Xenophon and strangled it. . . . I confess it cost me a severe struggle to relinquish the fond dream . . . but abler hands snatched it from my weak womanly fingers and waved me to humbler paths of labor."[66] Suppressing her own ambitions to write nonfiction under the cover of condoned gender conventions, Evans placed her hopes on the same altar of sacrifice that she detailed in *Macaria.*

But her decision was just as likely influenced by her assessment of the market. Recognizing that Stephens's history would probably outsell hers, she chose to stay within her own niche and further enhanced her proven track record in the fiction market. Negotiating between the demand for compelling stories and the need for both Evans and her readers to distance themselves from the past, the multiple editions of *Macaria* become expert witnesses to the complexity of the past. The testimony they provide shows us that their durability was tied not simply to their readability but rather to their supposed applicability. Multiple editions, like the born-digital, are residual artifacts, record keepers and markers of a particular moment in time and space. Like the digital media they portend, editions bear the imprint of their time and place while enduring beyond the purely ephemeral. *Macaria*'s sophisticated rhetorical strategies reflect Evans's understanding—and manipulation—of what James Machor calls "socialized patterns of interpretations."[67] As with her contemporary (and literary adversary) Harriet Beecher Stowe, whose humanitarian realism was meant to galvanize readers into social action, Evans's humanitarian sentimentalism is meant to return its readers to a romanticized past and, she hoped, restore it. She counts on the relativism that is part and parcel of the reading experience—and the tools of the trade for the novelist—to do the work of argument. Hers is a soft sell, especially in contrast to the hard sell of *Uncle Tom's Cabin.* Evans's inflections of sentimentalism unravel Northern prejudices against the South in part by eschewing explicit discussion of slavery and focusing instead on the larger framework of constitutional justice and the impact Northern aggression is having on the Southern family.[68]

Macaria and the study of multiple editions reveal that the mutability, customizability, and inherent sociability of electronic texts are already part of the way we experience texts: a preexisting textual condition. Studying multiple editions allows us to track networks and topologies of reading, as in James Green's discovery that merchant marines were the principal readers of Olaudah Equiano's narrative through the tracing of multiple copies to a bookseller in Newburyport, Massachusetts.[69] Thus, though editions are indeed autonomous objects, they are far more mutable than the emphasis on their material condition would suggest. The story these multiple editions do not tell, however, is that of the role editors play in their production. For that story, we turn to another Southern woman: Mary Boykin Chesnut.

CHAPTER 5

Loss (Authorship Regained)

In previous chapters I have explored the effects of publication on defining authorship, limiting creativity, and shaping textual output in the literary careers of Jane Johnston Schoolcraft, Sojourner Truth, Hannah Crafts, and Augusta Evans. I have done so by taking up a series of discrete if nested terms typically associated with the history of the book. Recasting literacy, authorship, publication, and edition as (re)mediation, memory, history, and testimony creates considerable traction for moving beyond the limitations of an oversimplified literary vocabulary that has become deceptively concrete. Thus far, however, my discussion has sidestepped Michel Foucault's assertion that "we can easily imagine a culture where discourse would circulate without any need for an author."[1] Although Foucault's "death of the author" has become a critical commonplace among philosophers of language and poststructural theorists, it still faces varying degrees of denial in literary studies. For historians of the book, especially, the author is the necessary agent of the work. But if we substitute "editor" for "author," we transform Foucault's avowal from a provocatively counterintuitive epiphany to a statement of the obvious. While editors have shaped literary history for centuries, albeit often silently, today's easy access to direct publication streams might seem to make them superfluous, like a book jacket on a Kindle.

In this chapter, however, I argue that the twenty-first-century editorial function needs as much, if not more, scrutiny if we are to come to terms with the transformative role editors play in texts. The functionality of software like CommentPress and PressBook that allows authors to shift their texts perpetually according to the ebb and flow of comments hardly eradicates the editor as negotiator, shaper, and judge;[2] rather, the editor, no longer a single viewpoint, is multiply present and utterly transparent in the form of the readers whose comments inform the text, framing it in the digital margins of the screen or backing it up in the page's history. In other words, the digital trend is toward multiauthored textual development that preserves everything, forever. A Google search for the term "editor" yields not the person but sources for editing, the service an editor provides. As with the citizen journalists armed with smart phones who collectively report events as they happen on Twitter and blogs, the shift away from (expert, univocal) editors mirrors the shift away from (expert, univocal) authors. What matters is the work, not the worker (or the worker's status), that is, the verb, not the noun.[3]

Taking up the question of the editor, this chapter focuses on the textual configurations of Mary Boykin Chesnut, whose literary status owes much to editorial intervention. Not quite a modern-day Thucydides in petticoats and pearls, Chesnut nonetheless has remained an essential source on the Civil War from the Southern perspective. She began writing during the Civil War, using a diary format both to keep track of events around her and to record her unconventional reactions to them. At the urging of Jefferson Davis's wife, Varina, Chesnut revised for publication but never actually published, believing her text was not yet ready for public consumption. She finally appeared in print for the first time in 1905, thanks to the efforts of her literary executor, Isabella D. Martin, and editor Myrta Avary. "The Diary From Dixie by Mary Boykin Chesnut" was initially serialized in the *Saturday Evening Post*, and *A Diary From Dixie* appeared soon thereafter in book form.[4] A diary in form if not in fact, the book and its title cast Chesnut's artistry as the voice of a war-ravaged Southern lady rather than the work of a sophisticated narrator. Varina Davis predicted that the diary's success would rival that of the then popular Southern plantation novelists, and she was right: its three major editions have garnered impressive sales figures, and the 1981 edition by the historian C. Vann Woodward won a Pulitzer Prize.[5]

Like Thoreau's *Journals*, Chesnut's so-called diary is almost as interesting for its complex provenance as for the history it covers.[6] A second edition, appreciably expanded, came out in 1949 under the same title. In 1982, Woodward freed the text of its impostor status as a diary, and today it is known as *Mary Chesnut's Civil War.* What characterizes all the iterations of what I will refer to as the Diary is that they were produced as much by editorial projections as by Chesnut's authorship. In this framework, each edition becomes not a replica but a numerical exponent of the Diary Chesnut originally wrote.[7] And, as I suggest in this chapter, each editor operates as his or her version's variable, exponentially transforming the text; from its first publication in the *Saturday Evening Post* in 1905 (Diary^{1}), to Diary^{2} published later that year, Diary^{3} in 1949, and Diary^{4} in 1981, each new edition raises the Diary to the next power.[8]

The Diary's complex publication history adds further insights to my discussion, in earlier chapters, of how publication can deform a text. Both 1905 publications, the *Saturday Evening Post* serialization (Diary^{1}) and the freestanding volume (Diary^{2}), reflect the remedial efforts of post-Reconstruction politics, offering the South redemption and the North revision. The Diary^{3} of 1949 burnishes a memory of the South primed in the late 1930s by the novel and film versions of *Gone With the Wind.* C. Vann Woodward's Diary^{4} is a triumph of editor over author, history over narrative. Chesnut's Diary is thus valuable not just for the story it tells us about its subject matter, but for its story about publication and the book as a cultural formation.

Unlike Hannah Crafts's, Chesnut's identity and status have never been disputed, nor has the authenticity of her narrative been doubted. Instead, the difficulties surrounding it stem from confusion over its textual identity, as the pages she originally wrote were worked and reworked, first by herself, then by multiple editors, shifting not just generically and stylistically, but even in such fundamental markers as title and length. Examination of this print history allows us to approach authorship from its margins. None of the editions is a stable text fully authorized by Chesnut herself. Rather, close analysis of the Diary(^{1,2,3,4}) illuminates how Chesnut's editors in effect became writers, selecting material and focusing it according to their own narrative principles, even as they maintained Chesnut's status as "author"; in other words, the focus shifts from authorial intention to its flip side, editorial intervention.[9] In essence, the

Diary's editors have turned the text into another palimpsest that serves as a public record of our efforts to (re)mediate, remember, historicize, and testify to the South's unsteady relationship to the literary history of the United States.

Chesnut's long-term cultural significance derives in large part from her place in history and resulting perspective.[10] As the wife of a South Carolina Confederate officer and confidante to many prominent Confederates, including Varina Davis, she was privy to much inside information. Chesnut was on hand when the first shots of the war were fired on Fort Sumter and when Grant devastated Richmond. But her eyewitness accounts are only part of her text's appeal; equally engaging—and historically worthwhile—are her biting assessments of the people, places, and events she experiences. In other words, like Crafts's novel, Chesnut's text depends intensely on the identity of its author.

The multiple iterations of Chesnut's Diary offer important insight into the formal features that constitute the concepts "book," "author," and "editor." Whereas others have read the various editions for narrative inconsistencies, in this chapter I take the Diaries as discrete expressions, a series of related items that are not causally connected, much like a series of whole numbers or integers.[11] And just as adding, subtracting, and multiplying any integer by an integer can only produce another integer, so I argue, following Jerome McGann's insight that "producing editions is one of the ways we produce literary meanings," that all of the print iterations, along with the extant manuscript texts, are equally "whole" and important elements of the archive.[12]

Part of the complexity of the Diary's publication history has to do with the unstable condition of the Diary itself. Indeed, tracing the history of Chesnut's initial Diary is a little like peeling an onion: once you've finished, there's nothing left. We have several versions of the original, but none of the materials that remain in the archive constitute a fair "copy-text" by any standards.[13] Instead these pages are the radical x factor, or root, that generates multiple integers, discrete wholes that derive from a complex of sources rather than simply fractions of the Diary. We also have a problem with textual coherence. From Isabella Martin to C. Vann Woodward, editors have faced a motley collection of handwritten notebooks, separate sheets, and revised books in the author's hand, none of them complete or authorized. Indeed, Chesnut asserted her authority in part through deletion: she destroyed all but three of the original wartime diaries once she completed her first edit. Unable to piece these parts together into any kind of originary whole, we are left, at the start, with a series of composites.

Chesnut herself understood the disparity between the elements that made up her Diary. The Diary refers to events during the war as memoir, calling attention to an important distinction between two discrete discourses and forms that have intertwined since diaries became a published genre.[14] Formally and methodologically, her canny reading of genre is one of the more interesting aspects of the Diary. Though Chesnut wrote a "diary," that is not what she intended to publish. She did not begin recording her thoughts on paper until February 1861. She marked the onset of the Civil War not with the firing on Fort Sumter but with the election of Abraham Lincoln and the secession of South Carolina. As a member of the Southern aristocracy, she declared, "I am by necessity a rebel born."[15] Over time, she accords herself few of the ordinary luxuries of the diarist. "I do not allow myself vain regrets or sad foreboding," she writes. Instead, she believed that the times called for "calm determination and cool brains."[16] In this initial entry, too, Chesnut recognizes the evidentiary value of her writing, observing, "I have seen, heard and forgotten so much—that again I must regret not keeping a daily record."[17] Her self-chastising remarks may be conventional, yet these comments suggest the complexity of Chesnut's project from its very beginning, though as time goes on, the notion of a record or chronicle becomes less important than the larger narrative trajectory.

By the 1870s, Chesnut was no longer simply keeping a record or even writing a diary: she was revising a book, though just what kind of book remains unclear. Chesnut put enormous energy and time into her revisions, transforming the diary into much more than a daily chronicle of events and thoughts. Her goal could have been to market the book as a history of the Civil War, for which there was a lively market.[18] Varina Davis believed that Chesnut's book held special promise in this realm. "I think your diaries," she wrote to Chesnut in 1885, "would sell better than any Confederate history of a grave character."[19] There were many possible publication outlets by the 1870s. *Appleton's Journal*, *Lippincott's Magazine*, and *Scribner's Monthly* opened up the market and welcomed Southern writers, and these broadening publishing opportunities brought a glut of stories by Southern women writers seeking to supplement family income.[20] Not surprisingly, this burgeoning industry produced a Southern counterpart to Hawthorne, Paul Hamilton Hayne, whose 1874 essay "Literature at the South: The Fungus School" offered a scathing assessment of their literary production and domination of the Southern literary marketplace. As his title heralds, he likened the spread of women's writing to the growth of spores, spreading as mold does in the dark and damp.[21] Given these circumstances, even Elisabeth Muhlenfeld, Chesnut's biographer, believes it was better for Chesnut herself and for literary history that she did not publish the diary in her lifetime. Like Schoolcraft and Crafts, by retaining formal control via *not* publishing, Chesnut "avoided both the defensiveness and sentimentalizing of the writers of her generation."[22]

The shrewdness of her decision becomes evident in her approach to revision. As late as 1883, three years before she died, Chesnut wrote to Varina Davis: "How I wish you could read over my journal. I have been two years overlooking it—copying—leaving myself out. You must see it—before it goes into print—but that may not be just now. I mean the printing—for I must overhaul it again—and again."[23] Chesnut struggled to strike a balance between the personalized narrative perspective of the diary form and a degree of objectivity that would give her views the purchase for which she longed.[24] She was not able to complete the job to her satisfaction, so we cannot know how she envisioned her final product. Instead we have what others created to make her work available to readers.

N. Katherine Hayles would likely identify Chesnut as a case of what she calls "remediated authorship"; that is, Mary Boykin Chesnut, author, is "a literary invention foregrounding the proliferation of inscription technologies that evacuate consciousness as the source of production and recover in its place a mediated subjectivity that cannot be conceived as an independent entity."[25] Thus Chesnut's work cannot be taken as a historical relic or naïve record, but must be understood as a highly mediated interpretation not just of her times, but of the narrative forms that dominated it. Chesnut's expressed hope that Varina Davis could see her work "before it goes into print" shows that she understood the process of print and publication as already remediating her writing through the lens of authorship. Her sense of urgency suggests her awareness of the difference between the diary as a personal form and the book as a public one, while her anxiety and reluctance about preparing the diary for publication indicate an understanding that the fluidity she gained through the diary form would be lost in print. Her fear seems well grounded as we observe, in the various print iterations of the Diary, the ongoing process of remediation between South and North that Chesnut hoped she might forestall. And as we trace each of these iterations, we also see how her text, by virtue of its unfinished quality, does retain a degree of the fluidity that was at the heart of her artistic vision. But no text can materialize outside of its material conditions, and each publication of the Diary emerges from and responds to particular historical conditions. Although the unpublished diary remains in fragmentary process, with each iteration, as the "diary" becomes the Diary^{1,2,3,4}, its meanings increase exponentially.

Exponential Developments: From Diary to Diary^1 and Diary^2

Chesnut's Civil War "Diary from Dixie" made its first appearance in 1905, edited by Isabella D. Martin and Myrta Lockett Avary, published initially in the *Saturday Evening Post*, which ran five serialized excerpts, and later in book form. The first *Saturday Evening Post* installment of "A Diary from Dixie," headed by an illustration of the firing on Fort Sumter, garnered placement on the issue's front page. The simple lines of the drawing render the event in broad strokes (fig. 10). The details of the illustration are less important than its symbolism: billowing clouds of smoke bring the silhouetted fort into relief far away across the ocean, suggesting that distance is necessary for the viewer and reader to appreciate this story. The absence of a caption implies that the reader is familiar with the event; indeed, at the outset of the war, *Harper's Weekly* featured a smoldering Fort Sumter on its cover, providing an iconic reference for the *Post*'s striking image.

George Lorimer, editor of the *Saturday Evening Post*, selected both the article's title and the accompanying illustration. Lorimer marketed the magazine as a "national weekly," and his editorial choices provide useful indications of his perceived audience.[26] In the first installment of the Diary^1, readers meet Chesnut—and the rest of the South—in a state of transition, both literally and figuratively. With a characteristically wry

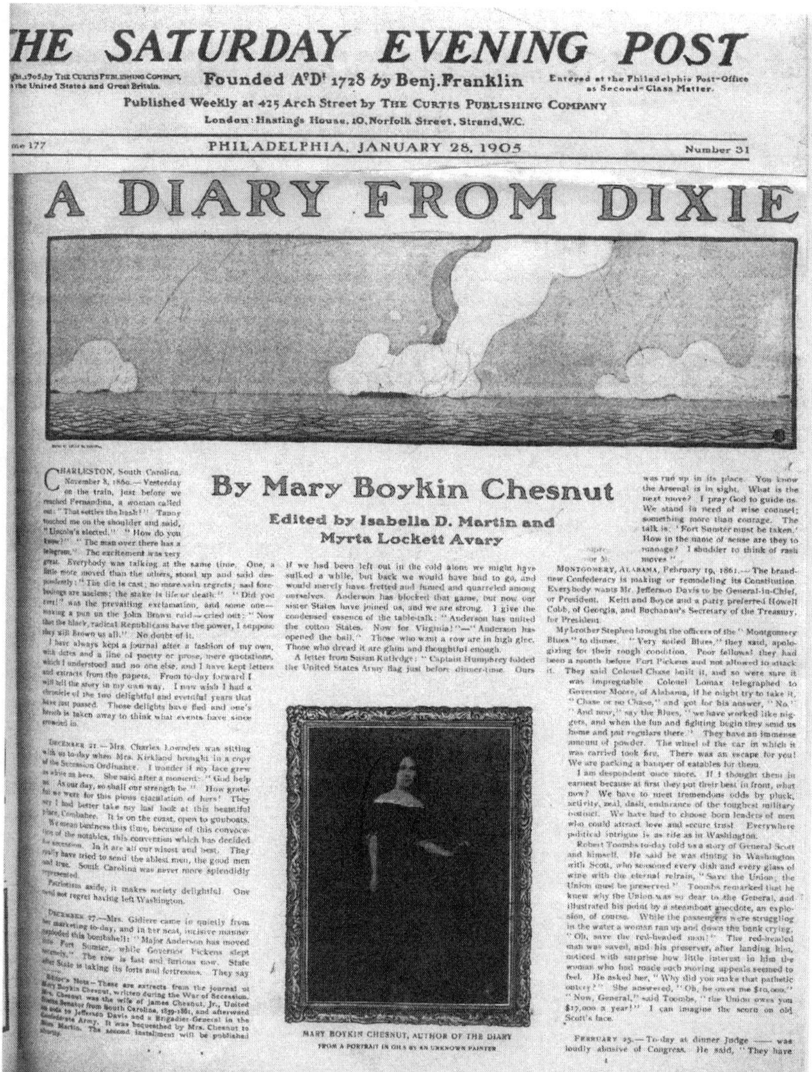

HE SATURDAY EVENING POST

ght, 1905, by The Curtis Publishing Company, the United States and Great Britain. Founded A°D¹ 1728 by Benj. Franklin. Entered at the Philadelphia Post-Office as Second-Class Matter.

Published Weekly at 425 Arch Street by The Curtis Publishing Company

London: Hastings House, 10, Norfolk Street, Strand, W.C.

me 177 PHILADELPHIA, JANUARY 28, 1905 Number 31

A DIARY FROM DIXIE

By Mary Boykin Chesnut

Edited by Isabella D. Martin and Myrta Lockett Avary

CHARLESTON, South Carolina, November 8, 1860.—Yesterday on the train, just before we reached Fernandina, a woman called out: "That settles the hash!" Tanny touched me on the shoulder and said, "Lincoln's elected." "How do you know?" "The man over there has a telegram." The excitement was very great. Everybody was talking at the same time. One, a little more moved than the others, stood up and said despondently: "The die is cast; no more vain regrets; sad forebodings are useless; the stake is life or death." "Did you ever!" was the prevailing exclamation, and some one—making a pun on the John Brown raid—cried out: "Now that the black, radical Republicans have the power, I suppose they will Brown us all." No doubt of it.

I have always kept a journal after a fashion of my own, with dates and a line of poetry or prose, mere quotations, which I understood and no one else, and I have kept letters and extracts from the papers. From to-day forward I will tell the story in my own way. I now wish I had a chronicle of the two delightful and eventful years that have just passed. Those delights have fled and one's breath is taken away to think what events have since crowded in.

December 21.—Mrs. Charles Lowndes was sitting with us to-day when Mrs. Kirkland brought in a copy of the Secession Ordinance. I wonder if my face grew as white as hers. She said after a moment: "God help us. As our day, so shall our strength be." How grateful we were for this pious ejaculation of hers! They say I had better take my last look at this beautiful place, Combahee. It is on the coast, open to gunboats.

We mean business this time, because of this convocation of the notables, this convention which has decided for secession. In it are all our wisest and best. They really have tried to send the ablest men, the good men and true. South Carolina was never more splendidly represented.

Patriotism aside, it makes society delightful. One need not regret having left Washington.

December 27.—Mrs. Gidiere came in quietly from her marketing to-day, and in her neat, incisive manner exploded this bombshell: "Major Anderson has moved into Fort Sumter, while Governor Pickens slept serenely." The row is fast and furious now. State after State is taking its forts and fortresses. They say if we had been left out in the cold alone we might have sulked a while, but back we would have had to go, and would merely have fretted and fumed and quarreled among ourselves. Anderson has blocked that game, but now our sister States have joined us, and we are strong. I give the condensed essence of the table-talk: "Anderson has united the cotton States. Now for Virginia!"—"Anderson has opened the ball." Those who want a row are in high glee. Those who dread it are glum and thoughtful enough.

A letter from Susan Rutledge: "Captain Humphrey folded the United States Army flag just before dinner-time. Ours was run up in its place. You know the Arsenal is in sight. What is the next move? I pray God to guide us. We stand in need of wise counsel; something more than courage. The talk is, 'Fort Sumter must be taken.' How in the name of sense are they to manage? I shudder to think of rash moves."

Editor's Note—These are extracts from the journal of Mary Boykin Chesnut, written during the War of Secession. Mrs. Chesnut was the wife of James Chesnut, Jr., United States Senator from South Carolina, 1859-1861, and afterward an aide to Jefferson Davis and a Brigadier-General in the Confederate Army. It was bequeathed by Mrs. Chesnut to Miss Martin. The second installment will be published shortly.

Montgomery, Alabama, February 19, 1861.—The brand-new Confederacy is making or remodeling its Constitution. Everybody wants Mr. Jefferson Davis to be General-in-Chief, or President. Keitt and Boyce and a party preferred Howell Cobb, of Georgia, and Buchanan's Secretary of the Treasury, for President.

My brother Stephen brought the officers of the "Montgomery Blues" to dinner. "Very soiled Blues," they said, apologizing for their rough condition. Poor fellows! they had been a month before Fort Pickens and not allowed to attack it. They said Colonel Chase built it, and so were sure it was impregnable. Colonel Lomax telegraphed to Governor Moore, of Alabama, if he might try to take it, "Chase or no Chase," and got for his answer, "No." "And now," say the Blues, "we have worked like niggers, and when the fun and fighting begin they send us home and put regulars there." They have an immense amount of powder. The wheel of the car in which it was carried took fire. There was an escape for you! We are packing a hamper of eatables for them.

I am despondent once more. If I thought them in earnest because at first they put their best in front, what now? We have to meet tremendous odds by pluck, activity, zeal, dash, endurance of the toughest military instinct. We have had to choose born leaders of men who could attract love and secure trust. Everywhere political intrigue is as rife as in Washington.

Robert Toombs to-day told us a story of General Scott and himself. He said he was dining in Washington with Scott, who seasoned every dish and every glass of wine with the eternal refrain, "Save the Union; the Union must be preserved." Toombs remarked that he knew why the Union was so dear to the General, and illustrated his point by a steamboat anecdote, an explosion, of course. While the passengers were struggling in the water a woman ran up and down the bank crying, "Oh, save the red-headed man!" The red-headed man was saved, and his preserver, after landing him, noticed with surprise how little interest in him the woman who had made such moving appeals seemed to feel. He asked her, "Why did you make that pathetic outcry?" She answered, "Oh, he owes me $10,000." "Now, General," said Toombs, "the Union owes you $17,000 a year!" I can imagine the scorn on old Scott's face.

February 25.—To-day at dinner Judge —— was loudly abusive of Congress. He said, "They have

[illegible]

MARY BOYKIN CHESNUT, AUTHOR OF THE DIARY

FROM A PORTRAIT IN OILS BY AN UNKNOWN PAINTER

[illegible]

Figure 10. Front-page illustration, *Saturday Evening Post*, January 28, 1905.

"That settles the hash," Chesnut describes hearing of Lincoln's election while on a train bound for Charleston. The entry clarifies the tension between the event depicted in the illustration and the title bestowed by the editor. The sectional ideological differences were heightened by Lincoln's election, which, as Chesnut makes clear, was, for the South, the true harbinger of war. Lincoln's election seemed to secure Northern interests and affirm Northern—that is, federal—political structures and power in a way that could only be addressed by war. Thus, if the shots fired on Fort Sumter served as the Northern marker of war, Lincoln's election signified battle for the South. From the very outset, then, the presentation of the Diary to a reading public preserves sectional differences by bringing these two versions of history together.

Bridging the gap was precisely the editor's goal. Unlike the "bloated" periodicals against which Augusta Evans railed, the *Saturday Evening Post* reflected Lorimer's particular vision, which in turn guided his selection of content.[27] According to his biographer, "Lorimer's aim was a magazine for no class, clique, or section, but for every adult mind in the then population of 75,000,000. . . . He set out to interpret America to itself, always readably, but constructively."[28] Commissioning the iconic illustration of Fort Sumter as a visual link to the narrative of Lincoln's election demonstrates Lorimer's ability to suture a war-torn readership. Treating his magazine as a "collective text," Lorimer understood reader dynamics in precisely the terms Clifford Geertz calls "deep play" (see chapter 4). Allowing illustrations to comment on the text and vice versa, he succeeded in bringing together North and South without simply collapsing them.

Lorimer soft-pedaled Chesnut's work to his newly imagined national readership in other ways as well. Moved back to page six in the next issue, the second installment's illustration once again suggests the angle that the text urges readers to take (fig. 11). This time the narrative is accompanied by a triptych that creates a sacred mood. The center panel depicts a genteel (as indicated by her position and attire) woman visiting a bedridden soldier. The scene could be set anywhere, except that the palmetto fan unmistakably indicates the South. The two side panels mirror each other formally, showing armed Confederate soldiers—on guard? in defeat? both?—with their heads bowed in deference to the scene between them. These excerpts begin with Chesnut's favorite nephew, who served as the model for the hero of her novel *The Captain and the Colonel*, leaving for the war. Though readers will not encounter him on his deathbed, the illustration anticipates his demise in serial fashion.[29] The serial places both a real and an imagined emphasis on the temporal, allowing us to focus our attention on the time and space of lived experience—as the

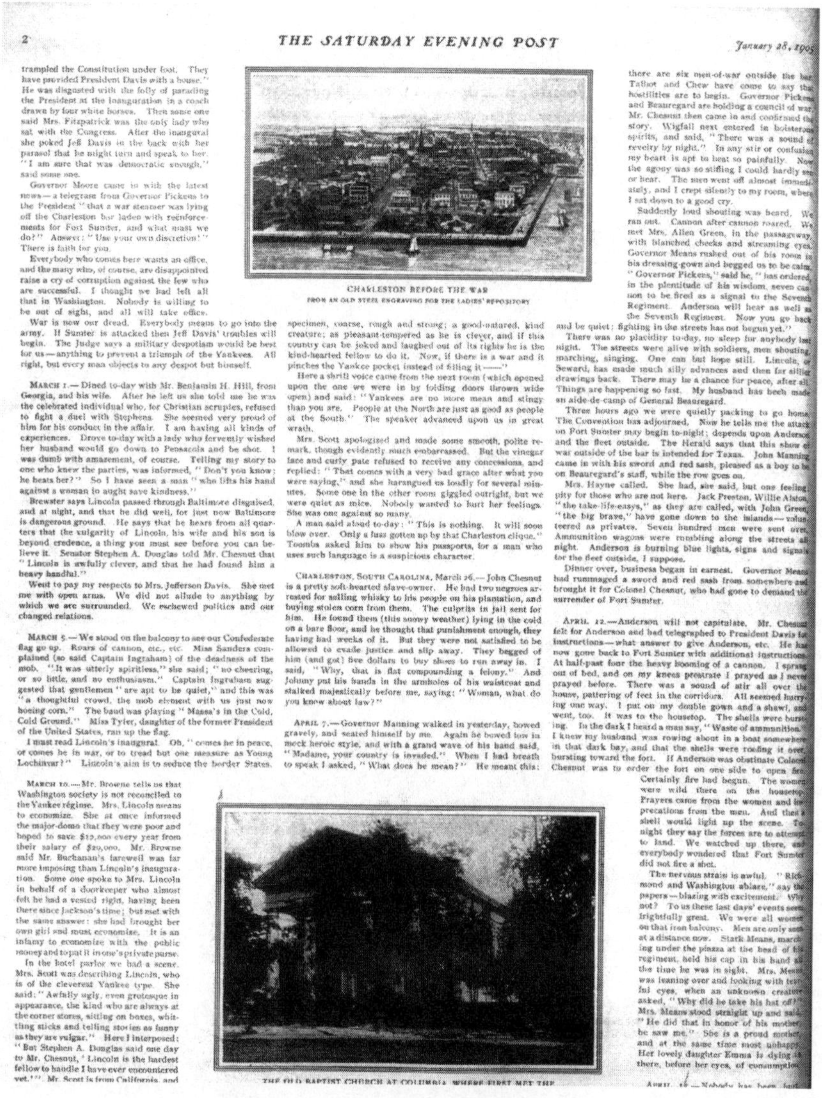

2 THE SATURDAY EVENING POST January 28, 1905

trampled the Constitution under foot. They have provided President Davis with a house." He was disgusted with the folly of parading the President at the inauguration in a coach drawn by four white horses. Then some one said Mrs. Fitzpatrick was the only lady who sat with the Congress. After the inaugural she poked Jeff Davis in the back with her parasol that he might turn and speak to her. "I am sure that was democratic enough," said some one.

Governor Moore came in with the latest news—a telegram from Governor Pickens to the President "that a war steamer was lying off the Charleston bar laden with reënforcements for Fort Sumter, and what must we do?" Answer: "Use your own discretion!" There is faith for you.

Everybody who comes here wants an office, and the many who, of course, are disappointed raise a cry of corruption against the few who are successful. I thought we had left all that in Washington. Nobody is willing to be out of sight, and all will take office.

War is now our dread. Everybody means to go into the army. If Sumter is attacked then Jeff Davis' troubles will begin. The Judge says a military despotism would be best for us—anything to prevent a triumph of the Yankees. All right, but every man objects to any despot but himself.

MARCH 1.—Dined to-day with Mr. Benjamin H. Hill, from Georgia, and his wife. After he left us she told me he was the celebrated individual who, for Christian scruples, refused to fight a duel with Stephens. She seemed very proud of him for his conduct in the affair. I am having all kinds of experiences. Drove to-day with a lady who fervently wished her husband would go down to Pensacola and be shot. I was dumb with amazement, of course. Telling my story to one who knew the parties, was informed, "Don't you know; he beats her?" So I have seen a man "who lifts his hand against a woman in aught save kindness."

Brewster says Lincoln passed through Baltimore disguised, and at night, and that he did well, for just now Baltimore is dangerous ground. He says that he hears from all quarters that the vulgarity of Lincoln, his wife and his son is beyond credence, a thing you must see before you can believe it. Senator Stephen A. Douglas told Mr. Chesnut that "Lincoln is awfully clever, and that he had found him a heavy handful."

Went to pay my respects to Mrs. Jefferson Davis. She met me with open arms. We did not allude to anything by which we are surrounded. We eschewed politics and our changed relations.

MARCH 5.—We stood on the balcony to see our Confederate flag go up. Roars of cannon, etc., etc. Miss Sanders complained (so said Captain Ingraham) of the deadness of the mob. "It was utterly spiritless," she said; "no cheering, or so little, and no enthusiasm." Captain Ingraham suggested that gentlemen "are apt to be quiet," and this was "a thoughtful crowd, the mob element with us just now hoeing corn." The band was playing "Massa's in the Cold, Cold Ground." Miss Tyler, daughter of the former President of the United States, ran up the flag.

I must read Lincoln's inaugural. Oh, "comes he in peace, or comes he in war, or to tread but one measure as Young Lochinvar?" Lincoln's aim is to seduce the border States.

MARCH 10.—Mr. Browne tells us that Washington society is not reconciled to the Yankee régime. Mrs. Lincoln means to economize. She at once informed the major-domo that they were poor and hoped to save $12,000 every year from their salary of $20,000. Mr. Browne said Mr. Buchanan's farewell was far more imposing than Lincoln's inauguration. Some one spoke to Mrs. Lincoln in behalf of a doorkeeper who almost felt he had a vested right, having been there since Jackson's time; but met with the same answer: she had brought her own girl and must economize. It is an infamy to economize with the public money and to put it in one's private purse.

In the hotel parlor we had a scene. Mrs. Scott was describing Lincoln, who is of the cleverest Yankee type. She said: "Awfully ugly, even grotesque in appearance, the kind who are always at the corner stores, sitting on boxes, whittling sticks and telling stories as funny as they are vulgar." Here I interposed: "But Stephen A. Douglas said one day to Mr. Chesnut, 'Lincoln is the hardest fellow to handle I have ever encountered yet.'" Mr. Scott is from California, and

CHARLESTON BEFORE THE WAR

FROM AN OLD STEEL ENGRAVING FOR THE LADIES' REPOSITORY

specimen, coarse, rough and strong; a good-natured, kind creature; as pleasant-tempered as he is clever, and if this country can be joked and laughed out of its rights he is the kind-hearted fellow to do it. Now, if there is a war and it pinches the Yankee pocket instead of filling it ——"

Here a shrill voice came from the next room (which opened upon the one we were in by folding doors thrown wide open) and said: "Yankees are no more mean and stingy than you are. People at the North are just as good as people at the South." The speaker advanced upon us in great wrath.

Mrs. Scott apologized and made some smooth, polite remark, though evidently much embarrassed. But the vinegar face and curly pate refused to receive any concessions, and replied: "That comes with a very bad grace after what you were saying," and she harangued us loudly for several minutes. Some one in the other room giggled outright, but we were quiet as mice. Nobody wanted to hurt her feelings. She was one against so many.

A man said aloud to-day: "This is nothing. It will soon blow over. Only a fuss gotten up by that Charleston clique." Toombs asked him to show his passports, for a man who uses such language is a suspicious character.

CHARLESTON, SOUTH CAROLINA, March 26.—John Chesnut is a pretty soft-hearted slave-owner. He had two negroes arrested for selling whisky to his people on his plantation, and buying stolen corn from them. The culprits in jail sent for him. He found them (this snowy weather) lying in the cold on a bare floor, and he thought that punishment enough, they having had weeks of it. But they were not satisfied to be allowed to evade justice and slip away. They begged of him (and got) five dollars to buy shoes to run away in. I said, "Why, that is flat compounding a felony." And Johnny put his hands in the armholes of his waistcoat and stalked majestically before me, saying: "Woman, what do you know about law?"

APRIL 7.—Governor Manning walked in yesterday, bowed gravely, and seated himself by me. Again he bowed low in mock heroic style, and with a grand wave of his hand said, "Madame, your country is invaded." When I had breath to speak I asked, "What does he mean?" He meant this:

there are six men-of-war outside the bar. Talbot and Chew have come to say that hostilities are to begin. Governor Pickens and Beauregard are holding a council of war. Mr. Chesnut then came in and confirmed the story. Wigfall next entered in boisterous spirits, and said, "There was a sound of revelry by night." In any stir or confusion my heart is apt to beat so painfully. Now the agony was so stifling I could hardly see or hear. The men went off almost immediately, and I crept silently to my room, where I sat down to a good cry.

Suddenly loud shouting was heard. We ran out. Cannon after cannon roared. We met Mrs. Allen Green, in the passageway, with blanched cheeks and streaming eyes. Governor Means rushed out of his room in his dressing-gown and begged us to be calm. "Governor Pickens," said he, "has ordered, in the plentitude of his wisdom, seven cannon to be fired as a signal to the Seventh Regiment. Anderson will hear as well as the Seventh Regiment. Now you go back and be quiet; fighting in the streets has not begun yet."

There was no placidity to-day, no sleep for anybody last night. The streets were alive with soldiers, men shouting, marching, singing. One can but hope still. Lincoln, or Seward, has made such silly advances and then far sillier drawings back. There may be a chance for peace, after all. Things are happening so fast. My husband has been made an aide-de-camp of General Beauregard.

Three hours ago we were quietly packing to go home. The Convention has adjourned. Now he tells me the attack on Fort Sumter may begin to-night; depends upon Anderson and the fleet outside. The Herald says that this show of war outside of the bar is intended for Texas. John Manning came in with his sword and red sash, pleased as a boy to be on Beauregard's staff, while the row goes on.

Mrs. Hayne called. She had, she said, but one feeling, pity for those who are not here. Jack Preston, Willie Alston, "the take-life-easys," as they are called, with John Green, "the big brave," have gone down to the islands—volunteered as privates. Seven hundred men were sent over. Ammunition wagons were rumbling along the streets all night. Anderson is burning blue lights, signs and signals for the fleet outside, I suppose.

Dinner over, business began in earnest. Governor Means had rummaged a sword and red sash from somewhere and brought it for Colonel Chesnut, who had gone to demand the surrender of Fort Sumter.

APRIL 12.—Anderson will not capitulate. Mr. Chesnut felt for Anderson and had telegraphed to President Davis for instructions—what answer to give Anderson, etc. He has now gone back to Fort Sumter with additional instructions. At half-past four the heavy booming of a cannon. I sprang out of bed, and on my knees prostrate I prayed as I never prayed before. There was a sound of stir all over the house, pattering of feet in the corridors. All seemed hurrying one way. I put on my double gown and a shawl, and went, too. It was to the housetop. The shells were bursting. In the dark I heard a man say, "Waste of ammunition." I knew my husband was rowing about in a boat somewhere in that dark bay, and that the shells were roofing it over, bursting toward the fort. If Anderson was obstinate Colonel Chesnut was to order the fort on one side to open fire. Certainly fire had begun. The women were wild there on the housetop. Prayers came from the women and imprecations from the men. And then a shell would light up the scene. To-night they say the forces are to attempt to land. We watched up there, and everybody wondered that Fort Sumter did not fire a shot.

The nervous strain is awful. "Richmond and Washington ablaze," say the papers—blazing with excitement. Why not? To us these last days' events seem frightfully great. We were all women on that iron balcony. Men are only seen at a distance now. Stark Means, marching under the piazza at the head of his regiment, held his cap in his hand all the time he was in sight. Mrs. Means was leaning over and looking with tearful eyes, when an unknown creature asked, "Why did he take his hat off?" Mrs. Means stood straight up and said, "He did that in honor of his mother; he saw me." She is a proud mother, and at the same time most unhappy. Her lovely daughter Emma is dying there, before her eyes, of consumption.

THE OLD BAPTIST CHURCH AT COLUMBIA, WHERE FIRST MET THE

Figure 11. Illustration, *Saturday Evening Post*, February 4, 1905.

reader must wait while writer, editor, or publisher doles out bite-sized pieces of narrative—and foregrounding the phenomenology of reading.

In addition to using drawings to create reader rapport, the *Post* also included many photographic reproductions of the people and places detailed in the Diary. One notable example in the first installment is a photo titled "Charleston Before the War" (fig. 12). In another effort to cultivate the reader's sentimental sweet tooth, the *Post* seems to be emphasizing loss by displaying the grandeur of the antebellum city. The photograph invites readers to envision the fall of Charleston and other major Southern cities as a consequence of the events depicted in the drawing that heads the installment. The publication context of a serial reveals the editor's importance in crafting reception through the publication process. Lorimer and the *Post* (unlike Martin and Avary) had less at stake in underscoring the Diary's historical accuracy than in promoting the reconciliation logic that sold copy.

Another important difference between the serial and book publications of *A Diary from Dixie* lies in their constructions of authorship. In the *Saturday Evening Post*, Chesnut appears as the author, as indicated in the byline "By Mary Boykin Chesnut." Immediately below the byline, in a smaller font, appear the words "Edited by Isabella D. Martin and Myrta Lockett Avary." Of the three names, only Avary's would have been known to readers, thanks to *A Virginia Girl in the Civil War, 1861–1865*, an edited collection she published in 1903 with D. Appleton. Ultimately, the text's author and editors matter less than its sensational subject matter, heralded by its title and illustration. Indeed, though each installment features an image of Chesnut, it is an image from an earlier time, "taken from a portrait in oils by an unknown painter."[30] Here again the relationship between text and accompanying image sets in motion an interpretive circuit. Both portrait and diary evoke the presence of the human hand rather than the mechanistic processes that generate the photograph and the printed text. The image suggests that the text too is idealized by the nostalgia now inherent in the protocols of its form and the technologies used to produce it.

The second incarnation of the Diary was as a book. As readers open this book, they encounter Chesnut. In place of an engraved image of the author, as was traditional with frontispieces, however, they find a photograph of the same oil portrait that appears in the *Saturday Evening Post* (fig. 13). Despite the existence of at least one photographic image on which to base an engraving, the editors chose to present Chesnut through the reproduction of a portrait, evoking the nostalgia of the older art form.[31] In keeping with the editors' original desire to title the book "With the Heroes of Dixie," this illustration presents Chesnut as a lady from

6 THE SATURDAY EVENING POST February 4, 190

A DIARY FROM DIXIE

By Mary Boykin Chesnut

CHARLESTON, SOUTH CAROLINA, May 28, 1861.—Johnny, my husband's nephew, has gone as a private in Gregg's regiment. He could not stand it at home any longer. Mr. Chesnut was willing for him to go, because those sandhill men said "this was a rich man's war," and the rich men would be the officers and have an easy time and the poor ones would be privates. So he said, "Let the gentlemen set the example; let them go in the ranks." So John Chesnut is a gentleman private. He took his servant with him all the same.

Johnny reproved me for saying, "If I were a man I would not sit here and dole and drink and drivel and forget the fight going on in Virginia." He said it was my duty not to talk so rashly and make enemies. He "had the money in his pocket to raise a company last fall, but it has slipped through his fingers, and now he is a common soldier." "You wasted it or spent it foolishly," said I. "I do not know where it has gone," said he. "There was too much consulting over me, too much good counsel was given to me, and everybody gave me different advice." "Don't you ever know your own mind?" "We shall do very well in the ranks; men and officers all alike; we know everybody," etc.

So I repeated Mrs. Lowndes' solemn words when she heard that South Carolina had seceded alone: "As thy days, so shall thy strength be." Don't know exactly what I meant, but thought I must be impressive as he was going away. Saw him off at the train. Forgot to say anything there, but cried my eyes out.

JUNE 4.—Mrs. Davis adores Mrs. Emory. No wonder I fell in love with her myself. I heard of her before I saw her in this wise. Little Banks told me the story. She was dancing at a ball when some bad accident maker for the Evening News rushed up and informed her that Major Emory had been massacred by ten Indians somewhere out West. She coolly answered him that she had later intelligence; it was not so. Turning a deaf ear then, she went on dancing. Next night the same officious fool met her with this congratulation: "Oh, Mrs. Emory, it was all a hoax. The Major is alive." She cried: "You are always running about with your bad news," and turned her back on him; or, I think it was, "You delight in spiteful stories," or, "You are a harbinger of evil." Banks is a newspaper man and knows how to arrange an anecdote for effect.

JUNE 10.—Have been looking at Mrs. O'Dowd as she burnished the "Meejor's arrms" before Waterloo. And I have been busy, too. My husband has gone to join Beauregard, somewhere beyond Richmond. I feel blue-black with melancholy. But I hope to be in Richmond before long myself. That is some comfort.

The war is making us all tenderly sentimental. No casualties yet, no real mourning, nobody hurt. So it is all parade, fife and fine feathers. Posing we are *en grande tenue*. There is no imagination here to forestall woe.

JUNE 19.—Mr. Chesnut is accused of firing the first shot, and his cousin, an ex-West Pointer, writes in a martial fury. They confounded the best shot made on the Island the day of the picnic with the first shot at Fort Sumter. This last is claimed by Captain James. Others say it was one of the Gibbeses who first fired. But it was Anderson who fired the train which blew up the Union. He slipped into Fort Sumter that night, when we expected to talk it all over.

Editor's Note—This is the second installment of these extracts from the War journal of Mrs. Chesnut, whose husband, a former Senator from South Carolina, was later an aide to Jefferson Davis, and prominent in the Confederacy. The third installment will be published in an early number.

MISS ISABELLA D. MARTIN
OWNER OF THE DIARY

RICHMOND, VIRGINIA, June 27.—Trescott was telling us how they laughed at little South Carolina in Washington. People said it was almost as large as Long Island, which is hardly more than a tailfeather of New York. Always there is a child who sulks and won't play; that was our rôle. And we were posing as San Marino; and all model-spirited, though small, republics pose.

He tells us that Lincoln is a humorist. Lincoln sees the fun of things; he thinks if they had left us in a corner or out in the cold a while pouting, with our fingers in our mouth, by hook or by crook he could have got us back; but Anderson spoiled all.

In Mrs. Davis' drawing-room last night the President took a seat by me on the sofa where I sat. He talked for nearly an hour. He laughed at our faith in our own powers. We are like the British. We think every Southerner equal to three Yankees, at least. We will have to be equivalent to a dozen now. After his experience of the fighting qualities of Southerners in Mexico, he believes that we will do all that can be done by pluck and muscle, endurance, and dogged courage, dash and red-hot patriotism, etc. And yet his tone was not sanguine. There was a sad refrain running through it all. For one thing, either way, he thinks it will be a long war. That floored me at once. It has been too long for me already. Then he said before the end came we would have many a bitter experience. He said only fools doubted the courage of the Yankees, or their willingness to fight when they saw fit. And now that we have stung their pride we have roused them till they fight like devils.

Mr. Lamar, who does not love slavery more than Sumner does, nor than I do, laughs at the compliment New England pays us. We want to separate from them; to be rid of the Yankees forever at any price. And they hate us so, and would clasp us, or grapple us, as Polonius has it, to their bosoms "with hoops of steel." We are an unwilling bride. I think incompatibility of temper began when it was made plain to us that we got all the opprobrium of slavery and they all the money there was in it with their tariff.

Mr. Lamar says the young men are light-hearted because there is a fight on hand, but those few who look ahead, the clear heads, they see all the risk, the loss of land, limb and life, home, wife and children. As in "the brave days of old," they take to it for their country's sake.

JUNE 28.—Mrs. Preston, Mrs. Wigfall, Mary Hammy and I drove in a fine open carriage to see the Champ de Mars. It was a grand tableau out there. Mr. Davis rode a beautiful gray horse, the Arab Edwin de Lion brought him from Egypt. His worst enemy will allow that he is a consummate rider, graceful and easy in the saddle, and Mr. Chesnut, who has talked horse with his father ever since he was born, owns that Mr. Davis knows more about horses than any man he has met yet. General Lee was there with him; also Joe Davis and Wigfall acting as his aides.

Poor Mr. Lamar has been brought from his camp—paralysis, or some sort of shock. Every woman in the house is ready to rush into the Florence Nightingale business. I think I will wait for a wounded man, to make my first effort as sister of charity. Mr. Lamar sent for me. As everybody went, Mr. Davis setting the example, so did I. Lamar will not die this time. Until their eyes close in death, will men flatter and make eyes at the ministering angels? He was the same old Lamar of the drawing-room.

JUNE 29.—As I was brushing flies away and fanning the prostrate Lamar to-day he said: "The fight had to come. We are men, not women. The quarrel had lasted long enough. We hate each other so, the fight had to come. Even Homer's heroes, after they had stormed and scolded enough, fought like brave men, long and well. If the athlete Sumner, had stood on his manhood and training, and struck back when Preston Brooks assailed him, Preston Brooks' blow need not have been the opening skirmish of the war. Sumner's country took up the fight because he did not. Sumner chose his own battlefield, and it was the worse for us. What an awful blunder that Preston Brooks business was." Lamar said Yankees did not fight for the fun of it; they always made it pay or let it alone.

Slavery has to go, of course, and joy go with it. These Yankees may kill us and lay waste our land for a while, but conquer us—never!

JULY 13.—We are always picking up some good thing of the rough Illinoisan's saying. Lincoln objects to some man—"Oh, he is too *interruptious*." That is a horrid style of man or woman, the interruptious. I know the thing, but had no name for it before.

Just now I happened to look up and saw Mr. Chesnut with a smile on his face watching me from the passageway. I flew across the room, and as I got half-way saw Mrs. Davis touch him on the shoulder. She said he was to go at once into Mr. Davis' room, where General Lee and General Cooper were. After he left us Mrs. Davis told me General Beauregard had sent Mr. Chesnut here on some army business.

JULY 14.—Mr. Chesnut remained closeted with the President and General Lee all the afternoon. The news does not se

Figure 12. "Charleston Before the War," *Saturday Evening Post,* January 28, 1905.

a bygone era. But the use of the portrait also calls attention to the constructed nature of the text itself. Emphasizing the simulation of authorship this text makes manifest in all its iterations, the portrait stands in contrast to the photographic realism of the traditional author frontispiece. As Roland Barthes observes, "Painting can feign reality without

MRS. JAMES CHESNUT, JR.
From a Portrait in Oil.

Figure 13. Portrait of Mary Chesnut from the *Saturday Evening Post,* reproduced in C. Vann Woodward edition, *Mary Chesnut's Civil War.* This portrait also appears in the 1906 Martin and Avary edition, *Diary from Dixie.* Image courtesy of Documenting the American South, The University of North Carolina at Chapel Hill Libraries.

having seen it"; so, too, *A Diary from Dixie* seems to say, a first-person account written in a stream-of-consciousness style can conjure reality through its representational choices.[32]

D. Appleton, Avary's New York publisher, brought out *A Diary from Dixie* under the rubric of "biography."[33] Much had changed at D. Appleton since its founder had rejected Evans's best-selling *Beulah.* W. H. Appleton, now at the company's helm, had a very different attitude than did his father toward the South and sectional differences. Like Lorimer at the *Post,* Appleton had seen the South firsthand, traveling there in 1865 as a young man to collect on accounts past due.[34] During that visit, he happened upon his first literary discovery and publishing success: work by Madame Louisa Muhlbach printed on straw paper. He recommended Muhlbach's novel for publication, and its sales ran into the millions.[35] Appleton's early involvement in publishing Southern authors also included the autobiography of General Joseph E. Johnston.[36]

Appleton's successes, and they were legion, stemmed from an uncanny ability to bring talent to market. He not only published Stephen Crane's novel *The Red Badge of Courage* but also, knowing what the market would bear, bowdlerized it and thus made it a best-seller.[37] Appleton also worked closely with authors. His editorial hand, transforming unintelligible academic jargon into a popular format, created a readership for the psychologist G. Stanley Hall, among many others.[38] Like Lorimer's, Appleton's goals were democratic in impulse. Indeed, despite his remarkable business acumen and market savvy, Appleton, like his father before him, staunchly supported an expanded and improved copyright law, resulting in the Copyright Act of 1891, and served as president of the Publishers' Copyright League for several years.[39] Chesnut, this ersatz author whose work seemed to belong at once to no one and everyone, offered him one more route to extend the ideological interests that marked his success in the publishing industry.

Though Appleton retained Lorimer's title, the book's title page reveals a different set of reader expectations that are deeply imbricated in the culture of the book (fig. 14). The title, *A Diary From Dixie,* appears in capital letters, followed by a comma and the phrase "as written by" in italic lowercase letters. From the mid-nineteenth century on, readers would have associated this phrase with another first-person narrative tradition: the slave narrative, which, as a form of protest against slavery, frequently identified literacy, emphatically announced by the phrase "as written by," as one of its most useful tools. Incorporating this freighted phrase links the Southern white woman with the Southern institution of plantation slavery while foregrounding Chesnut's literacy above all her other subsequently listed credentials, even her very name. Indeed, the phrase appears in the same line as "Dixie," the last word of the title. The top quarter of the cover, which contains the title, author, and author's credentials, is visually cluttered and increasingly difficult to read as the font shifts to ever smaller italics. When the names of editors Martin and Avary appear in bold letters of the same font size as Chesnut's name, surrounded by white space that draws the eye away from the block of text above, their prominence is firmly established. Appleton's publisher seal floating just below the names draws additional attention to the editors.

Isabella Martin, Chesnut's de facto literary executor, was a girl during the Civil War and one of Chesnut's younger friends. Martin is also a character in the Diary itself. Once Chesnut decided to entrust Martin with her diaries, however, she went back over the text, tweaking passages to portray Isabella heir as bright, feisty, and a fitting representative for her literary legacy: "Feb 22—Isabella has been reading my diaries. How we laugh because my sage diversions all come to naught. My famous 'insight into character' is utter folly. The diaries were lying on the hearth ready to be burned, but she told me to hold on to them; think of them a while and don't be rash" (*Diary* 1905, 350). The observations are the same in the original and revised entries, except that in the original Chesnut is the speaker. By putting her words in Isabella Martin's mouth, Chesnut was grooming her friend's "character" for her future editorial position. Despite the dictates of modesty that guided many of her other deletions, Martin let this text stand, and it appeared in the published edition.[40]

Chesnut's long-held ambition to publish her memoirs would not be realized until almost ten years after her death, when Martin met Myrta Avary, a writer with roots in the South, who had published *A Virginia Girl in the Civil War* (1903) as well as other short stories and poems. In 1905 Avary collaborated with Martin to prepare Chesnut's work for publication, an endeavor that also allowed her to realize her ambition to move away from fiction writing into history.[41] One way the Avary-Martin Diary calls attention to itself as history is through its footnotes, which put the text in a different epistemic relationship to the reader. Signaling

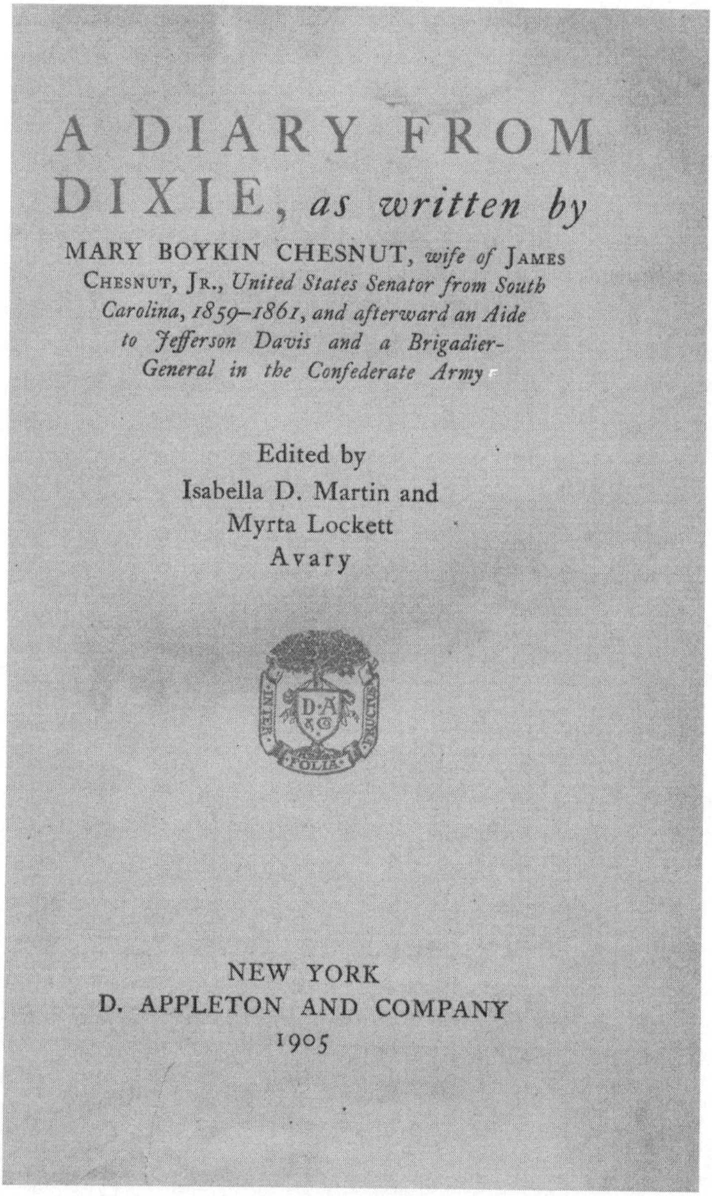

A DIARY FROM DIXIE, *as written by*
MARY BOYKIN CHESNUT, *wife of* JAMES CHESNUT, JR., *United States Senator from South Carolina, 1859–1861, and afterward an Aide to Jefferson Davis and a Brigadier-General in the Confederate Army*

Edited by
Isabella D. Martin and
Myrta Lockett
Avary

NEW YORK
D. APPLETON AND COMPANY
1905

Figure 14. Title page of *A Diary from Dixie, as written by Mary Boykin Chesnut,* edited by Isabella D. Martin and Myrta Lockett Avary, 1905. Image courtesy of Documenting the American South, The University of North Carolina at Chapel Hill Libraries.

their position as proprietors and professionals, their use of footnotes, for instance, to explain a reference to John Brown, remind the reader that Avary and Martin control the text as a material and historical object. Meditating on the power of the footnote to identify and legitimize authors and texts as serious work, Anthony Grafton equates "the low rumble of the footnote" with "the high whine of the dentist's drill," explaining that "the tedium [the footnote] inflicts, like the pain inflicted by the drill, is not random but directed, part of the cost that the benefits of modern science and technology exact."[42] Assuring readers of the text's legitimacy as a historical document, Avary and Martin's footnotes interrupt the pleasure of the text.

The *New York Times* recognized the volume's status as history by inviting William E. Dodd, a soon-to-be prominent historian of the South, to review it.[43] The review's headline, "Mrs. Chesnut's Diary," emphasizes both the author's marital status and the book's generic status. The review begins by acknowledging that although the market for books on the Civil War is oversaturated, "the demand for information about the war has not . . . been satisfied; each new volume meets with ready sale, and the story teller who can dress up the war heroes with a little romance and less historic incident is sure of his fortune and fame."[44] (Dodd's characterization of the market was spot-on, for the book sold briskly, and a weekly "Books and Authors" column in the same issue of the *Times* described it as "steadily in demand.")[45] Yet romancing the history of the war is hardly Dodd's main concern. Rather, he posits Chesnut's Diary in the context of a corrective. "We are all beginning to see," he observes, echoing the reconciliation logic of the era, "there was not all of right on one side nor all of wrong on the other. And as time goes on it will probably become clear that the war was one of the great stages in the evolution of 'democratic Government on the earth.'" But as much as he seems to value the book for its long-sightedness, he has trouble with its narrativity: "In tone and character this new war book is admirable, though, of course, there is no general scheme or plan or even purpose except to record the talk of the time with occasional expressions of personal views which in most cases are far from being tedious."[46] Clearly put off by the Diary's lack of linear narrative, Dodd somewhat reluctantly accepts its looseness as a condition of its form. If he had known more about its revision history, however, he might not have been so accepting.

Avary and Martin had planned on calling the Diary "With the Heroes of Dixie," proffering a distinctly pro-South perspective as a unifying narrative theme. Their edits, especially the deletions, make this theme even clearer. But it is unlikely that Dodd or the public ever knew of their intended title, nor would they have known that Chesnut herself revised heavily throughout the 1880s, after she wrote several unpublished novels. Her work on these fictional texts helped her enormously, giving her hands-on experience in resolving the very issues of narrativity that critics, historians, and readers have consistently admired.[47] Unbeknownst to all but her editors, Chesnut purposefully preserved the generic form of the diary while invisibly working a narrative trajectory into the text. Moving back and forth from narrative incident to narrative analysis, Chesnut's revised texts achieve the "readability" factor toward which her editors strove; this achievement results from the way her revisions marry the diary form to the conventions of fiction and narrativity. The resulting Diary thus has much in common with Thomas Dixon's 1905 bestseller *The Clansman*, without being subject to the romanticizing norms of plantation fiction.[48] She managed, in other words, to eschew plot in favor of story by maintaining the diary in the book.

The first-person diary narrative offered Chesnut other advantages. Polemics—about slavery, the North, and even *Uncle Tom's Cabin*—did not have to be fully incorporated into the larger narrative pattern of the book. Asides, tangents, and radical departures are simply part of the diary's stream of consciousness. The Diary does not suffer from problems generated by wooden characters or plot, as do Chesnut's three experiments in novel writing during the 1870s. On the contrary, the diary form enables her to preserve a degree of flexibility and ambivalence that made her work feel decidedly modern to later critics such as Edmund Wilson, Daniel Aaron, and C. Vann Woodward.[49] Critics have often used the example of her cousin Betsy Witherspoon's murder by her slaves to track the benefits of the diary form to the book's overall narrative success. In the 1905 edition, the reader learns of Witherspoon's death in the past tense: "*Sept 19th*.—A painful piece of news came to us yesterday—our cousin, Mrs. Witherspoon, of Society Hill, was found dead in her bed. She was quite well the night before. Killed, people say, by family sorrows" (*Diary* 1905, 129). This account portrays Betsy Witherspoon's death exclusively in sentimental terms, as a sad but relatively ordinary event. Readers would have to wait till 1949 to discover, in Diary[3], that Mrs. Witherspoon was killed by her slaves.

D³=Eavesdropping on History

Almost fifty years after Martin and Avary's edition, the Diary was edited by the novelist and screenwriter Ben Ames Williams, who had used it as a historical source for the Civil War South in his best-selling *House Divided* (1947).[50] Riding on the novel's success, Williams and his publisher, Houghton Mifflin, brought out the second edition of Chesnut's text in 1949. Though Williams preserved Lorimer's title, his version is double the length of the 1905 edition;[51] as he explains, the previous editors had left out precisely those sections he deemed "most interesting" (*Diary* 1949, xxiv). Williams's edition reflects a change in the text's purpose and proposed readership. For one thing, he promised to restore the Diary's chronicle aspect, to increase readability. He also believed that in its expanded form the Diary would reveal what he called "an undiscovered country" remarkable for what I've elsewhere called humanitarian realism: he felt that the travails of Mary Chesnut and her compatriots would have narrative impact and social relevance beyond their own circumstances (xxiv).[52] Unlike in the popularized South of *Gone With the Wind*, "here are men and women of flesh and blood," Williams writes in his introduction (xxiv). He sees Chesnut's figures as "infinitely more human in their faults and their fancies than the lay figures which march solemnly through the pages of so many books of fact or fiction dealing with the Southern scene" that modeled history on the narrative pattern of the romance (xxiv). His version of the Diary, in contrast, is shaped by the narrative model of tragedy, in which Chesnut learns and instructs the reader through the experience of her suffering.

Returning to the Witherspoon passage helps us glean a sense of Williams's editorial practices. Williams takes advantage of Chesnut's diary form by using it himself: in addition to the original entry dated "Sept 19th" that appeared in the earlier 1905 edition, he restores a subsequent entry removed by Avary and Martin: "*Sept 21st.*—Last night when the mail came in, I was seated near the lamp. Mr. Chesnut, lying on a sofa at a little distance, called out to me: 'Look at my letters and tell me who they are from?' I began to read one of them aloud. It was from Mary

Witherspoon, and I broke down; horror and amazement was too much for me. Poor cousin Betsy Witherspoon was murdered! She did not die peacefully in her bed, as we supposed, but was murdered by her own people, her Negroes" (139). The restored passage re-creates the shock and drama of the event by reporting it again, this time by means of a letter correcting the original account. Williams appends a footnote to this entry in which he suggests that its absence from the previous edition was due "presumably" to the missing notebooks, now found, correcting the record without correcting his predecessors. He justifies the shocking impact of the information with recourse to his historical mission, calling it "too important to any full picture of the South to be omitted."[53] Revisions like this one create what Hayden White calls "emplotment" by foregrounding chronology.[54] Emphasizing the lived nature of the diary by virtue of events presented in sequence forges links between art and life that highlight the importance of narrativity itself. Thus, though the 1949 Diary[3] offers a "tragic" model of history, it nevertheless still positions the text as an authentic diary left untouched by its author in her lifetime.[55]

The *New York Times* review of Williams's edition drilled down into the diary's authenticity. "This intimate record of the Civil War as set down by a witty South Carolina belle," says the reviewer, "is more enthralling than many a fat, romantic Civil War novel. We are all petty eavesdroppers. That's why biographies, published letters and diaries are so popular. Well, read Mrs. Chesnut's journal and eavesdrop to your heart's content." If the 1905 version emblematized its lost cause philosophy, as evoked in Martin and Avary's original title, "With the Heroes of Dixie," the 1949 edition foregrounded the idiosyncratic wit and elegance of a diary's private pages, which can be accessed only by eavesdropping.

Williams's choice to retain the diary form has additional effects as well. As Blakey Vermeule observes: "Gossip relentlessly favors some kinds of information over other kinds. Sexual scandal, cheating, sudden windfalls, dramatic successes, spectacular failures, and social climbing all take precedence over other kinds of information." This assessment aptly describes Chesnut's choices, in terms of both their content and their overall effect. As Vermeule further remarks: "Gossip is always concerned with power. It follows in the track of the great and never clings for very long to the down and out." It offers both the speaker and the listener a way out of their own circumstances. In other words, as Vermeule notes, "people gossip up." The narrative style in the 1949 edition of Chesnut's Diary in effect turns readers into intimates, listening to the gossip of history. At the same time, even as gossip attracts the listener/reader, it also has a particular power to repel: "We are willing to know information about others that we do not want known about ourselves. We are willing to engage in an activity that we do not want it known that we engage in—even gossiping turns out to be the sort of thing we wouldn't want known about ourselves."[56] The privacy created by book covers, the printed page, and a silent reader simulates the conditions needed for what Patricia Meyer Spacks calls "serious" gossip. According to Spacks, serious gossip "takes place in private, at leisure, in the context of trust, usually among no more than two or three people. . . . It provides a resource for the subordinated . . . a crucial means of self-expression, a crucial form of solidarity."[57] Williams's edition succeeds because it creates an alliance between Chesnut, the narrator who is prescient enough to be suspicious of slavery but human enough to want the status, frills, and fun provided by a slave economy, and readers nostalgic for the bygone era of *Gone With the Wind* and Diary^3.

D^4: Solving for X

In 1981, under the editorship of C. Vann Woodward, the Diary underwent its most radical revision yet, resulting in a hybrid edition that combined the Civil War texts Chesnut revised in the early 1880s with selections from the original diaries. Now titled *Mary Chesnut's Civil War*, Woodward's edition won a Pulitzer Prize for history. As the change in the title suggests, his edition moves the Diary away from the emplotment of previous versions, whether the South as romance (1905) or the tragedy of the South (1949). Instead Woodward fully restores the chronicle. As a result, though still fascinating, his Diary lacks the cohesion Chesnut labored to achieve, and thus becomes radically unreadable. As Julia Sterne has observed, the Woodward edition invites readers to see how Chesnut uses the miniature fragment for epic purposes.[58] It is precisely this quality that seems to render it a legitimate historical document. In this format, Chesnut is the citizen journalist, blogging from the scene of the event, building social relationships between historical events and the people these events concern.

The book is bulky beyond the wildest imaginings. Even Chesnut, who declared, "The scribbling mania is strong within me," would be astonished by its length (a whopping 892 pages) and, more than likely, dismayed by its lack of narrative elegance. All of her most intimate opinions of herself and others have been restored, no matter how crass or embarrassing. *Mary Chesnut's Civil War* gives new meaning to the terms "uncensored" and, perhaps more important, "unauthorized." Rendering Chesnut's literary efforts practically null, Woodward violates principles of authorship by printing material she edited out. Though we may not be able to answer the essential questions about authorship that Chesnut's case prompts, the multiple publications of her Diary are suggestive, even in the wake of Barthes, Foucault, and others. In these publications, she is as much an ersatz author as the South is an ersatz region layered over time. And as this analysis has shown, as the versions of the diary multiply, each provides an archaeology of its contemporary constructions of race, region, gender, and class as much as the historical record.

$X \leq D^1+D^2+D^3+D^4$: Life Beyond Biography, History Outside the Archive

None of the editions of Chesnut's Diary takes the values of literary editing, in which authorial intention remains primary, as its guiding principle. Rather, the goals of these editions are informed by history and historiography. Therefore, unlike Elisabeth Muhlenfeld, I will not return to the Diary to probe its status as a "remnant" or witness of authorship, that which remains between the Diary and the Diary^{1,2,3,4}.[59] To do so would be to imply that we might finally obtain the "real" diary by producing an eclectic edition based on the principle of preserving authorial intention and rigorous standards of critical editing. Instead I want to focus on a brief, discrete piece of Chesnut's archive, a short story excerpted from the Diary that she titled "The Bright Side of Richmond." Readers are invited to extrapolate from this example to the larger Diary by its subtitle, "Scraps from a Diary." This diary in miniature exposes Chesnut's strategies for revision and implies, perhaps more significantly than any of the extant Diary editions, an aesthetic principle that contemporary critics would liken to postmodern hypertext, in which authorship is radically mediated through a variety of technologies, and texts fundamentally violate the norms that divide and determine central concepts such as book, author, editor, edition, and the ever important reader.

Woodward believes that Chesnut polished the story "with a view to separate publication" (*MCCW,* 528n4). Although this hunch would be difficult to prove, the manuscript recalls one of Dickinson's fascicles in its intentional construction as a discrete piece of work. Two holes, where brass fasteners once stood, puncture the top edge of the packet, and the pages are, for the most part, consecutively numbered. The redundant pages seem to be manuscript pages in stages of revision; appearing toward the end of the packet, they suggest that, as was often the case, Chesnut had not quite finished her project.[60] There are indications, however, that she had finished the earlier pages of the manuscript, and Woodward believes it is the last thing she wrote.[61] On the strength of the story's integrity as a completed piece of writing, his team substituted it for the original diary pages that correspond to the same period "because it is clearer and better written" (*MCCW,* 528n4). "The Bright Side of Richmond" thus lets us get as close as we possibly can to a consideration of the nature of Chesnut's authorship, taking her writing not as a history but as a literary text vibrating with meaning through the signifying power of the poet.

The manuscript text of "The Bright Side of Richmond" may remind readers of Emily Dickinson in style as well as format. Like Dickinson, Chesnut routinely bends language, including rules of punctuation and capitalization, allowing the written text to be meaningful and fresh. As Jennifer DeVere Brody observes, "punctuation marks can serve as both sense and sensibility—as the most human element in certain sentences."[62] Chesnut uses punctuation, capitalization, and grammatically incomplete sentences to prevent her narrative from becoming any more routinized than the experiences she describes:

> 8th Snow of the deepest. Nobody can come today.
>
> But they did come. First of all. braving wind and weather – my girls. Then Constance Cary. The clever Cary – Hetty is the beauty – so called – but then Hetty has brains and to spare – and Constance has a classically perfect outline – How her adorers rave of that profile!. Then the four tall Kentuckians. and Preston Hampton as tall as any – and ~~ever~~ so much handsomer.

> JC came home – "Where are you going?"
>
> – "To take Constance Cary to Mrs Semmes charade party." He calmly asked the price of that carriage at the door – "$25 an hour" –
>
> – "Such extravagance – such stupid charades." He worked himself up – till he fairly swore by all his Gods – that the play was not worth the Candle" – "You mean carriage in this instance." Then he quieted down.
>
> – "After all in Confederate Money – it sounds so much worse than it is."

Opening this segment in diary-like fashion with the date, interspersing dialogue as if in a play, and editorializing from the point of view of an omniscient narrator, Chesnut freely merges generic features to create a fluid narrative that builds tension through pace and delivery. Chesnut's awareness that language is flexible is linked to her nuanced understanding of language as spoken. "'That,'" she explains, "as an American demonstrative adjective pronoun, or adjective pure and simple—we give it illimitable meaning. . . . A peculiar intonation, however, must be given to *that* to make it bear its mountain of meaning" (*MCCW*, 519). Calling upon readers to intone her meaning, she treats the diary form as closer to speech than to writing, anticipating the immediacy of the blog post. She understands that the printed text will be conditioned and censored by available formats: more rigorously "remediated," to return to Hayles's formulation. "The Bright Side of Richmond" reminds us that Chesnut believed in the writing process, as it approximates experience, but had reservations about the book as a formal category.

In "The Bright Side of Richmond," we see clearly Chesnut's efforts to concoct a stream-of-consciousness style that bridges the gap between the literary and the historical text. Thinking outside the book and its normative forms, Chesnut vacillated between the rhetorical demands of the nonfiction diary and the literary freedom of fiction, and in so doing ultimately "left herself out" of the authorial enterprise. Among the contemporary examples Chesnut must have considered, her friend Sue King's *Busy Moments of an Idle Woman* would not have escaped her notice. James Woods Davidson, author of *The Living Writers of the South* (1869), valued King's work highly: "Her books are all societal, sketchy, and full of French; about sore-hearted women and gay life, coquetry, ill-assorted loves, with worse-assorted lives; abounding in sharp and sparkling conversations and quarrels, racey repartees, and brilliant banter; manifesting constantly a tendency to the style known as gay and festive, with a strong *soupçon* of satire upon the conventional respectabilities, and with decided flavor of *mots à double entendre*."[63] This description captures Chesnut's aesthetic as well as King's and makes a clear case that neither her voice nor her formal efforts to preserve speech in writing are original. Yet her clear departures from standard grammar, punctuation, and capitalization, seen in "The Bright Side of Richmond" and all three editions of the Diary, resist the stabilizing force of textuality by positioning the Diary as testimony.

The philosopher Giorgio Agamben comments that testimony "guarantees not the factual truth of the statement safeguarded in the archive, but rather its unarchivability, its exteriority with respect to the archive—that is, the necessity by which, as the existence of language, it escapes both memory and forgetting."[64] Chesnut's efforts to preserve speech over writing in the face of a literacy-laden culture in which acts of authorship were rigidly controlled by print conventions can also be seen as an affirmation of "unarchivability" and a refusal to acquiesce to the limitations of those conventions. This affirmation and refusal coalesce with her wish to keep the diary form. What we have, then, in "The Bright Side of Richmond" and the various iterations of the Diary, is not the scraps of a book but rather the remnants of authorship.

Through repeated reading and republication, Chesnut's diary continues to contest and resist genre by imagining language as capable of existing outside normative generic forms. In line with Virginia Jackson's efforts to recalibrate our understanding of Emily Dickinson outside the lyric, we must see Chesnut outside the book.[65] Once we accept the state of her work as such, we can understand her reluctance to publish not as a form of perfectionism, nor as a simple fact of life, but rather as a rejection of the book as a controlling form and norm. Bequeathing her work to Isabella D. Martin might thus be considered a blatant attempt to establish co-authorship. Chesnut could not have anticipated that Martin, the feisty, fiery Southern belle, would turn her diaries over to Myrta Avary, whose claim to historiography was that she found her archive "among teacups."[66] I do not wish to bemoan the existence of any of the editions of the Diary, but I do want to restore a degree of intentionality to Chesnut's own work.

Agamben's question, "How can a subject give an account of its own ruin?" is at the heart of that work, preventing Chesnut from completing the project that would ultimately be the end of her.[67] Positing her Diary as it is allows us to take her artistry as a serious effort to think outside the book.

EPILOGUE

No Text Left Behind (A Theory of Recovery)

I conclude these ruminations with an evocative image from Miranda Maher's "Manipulated Books" series (fig. 15). Upon discovering a book that had fallen behind a dresser, Maher, an artist, noticed that "it had become permanently twisted into this beautiful spiraling shape."[1] In recognizing the new shape's distorted elegance rather than fixating on the damage, Maher mirrors the conceptual project at the heart of *Thinking Outside the Book*. Just as the 2009 MacArthur Foundation report on education and digital culture urged us to remain focused on human agency, so have I taken up digital media and culture not as a radical new paradigm but as an extension of earlier practices and a reciprocal force. In addition to developing an alternate typology for key literary and publishing concepts that have, in practice, long gone unchallenged in academic and popular circles, I have used this typology to produce a theory of recovery that takes into account the book as text and as work. In other words, in addition to treating the archives of my focal figures as texts, I have also considered their value as spiraling metatexts, emphasizing their ability to tell us as much about the making of literary history as they do about the literary in literary history.[2] "Archive" has served here as both noun and verb, a usage that in turn echoes digital products and processes.

Figure 15. "Witch Book" by Miranda Maher. Used by permission of the artist.

Recasting literacy, authorship, publication, edition, and editor as (re) mediation, memory, history, testimony, and loss has created considerable traction for moving beyond the limitations of an oversimplified vocabulary that has become deceptively concretized in the study of literary history. But underneath the need to broaden our conceptual vocabulary is the need to attend closely to the way recovery has fueled so much of literary studies since the nineteenth century. Indeed, many of the signature works in the field of nineteenth-century American literature, from the now canonical *Moby Dick* to Emily Dickinson's unpublished poetry, owe their existence to recovery, which, in its various stages, has defined and reinvented that field.

Walter Benjamin's reflections on the differences between historicism and historical materialism aptly frame recovery efforts in literary history. He writes, "The awareness that they are about to make the continuum of history explode is characteristic of the revolutionary classes at the moment of their action."[3] The historians, such as John Blassingame and Eugene Genovese, who recovered slave testimony as a legitimate historical source, were motivated by the burgeoning civil rights movement. Their work reconfigured the past, moving the slave experience from margin to center of the story of American history and historiography. These efforts resonated deeply across the intellectual landscape, opening the way for further recovery work in other fields. For literary studies, recovery work itself carried a revolutionary fervor, transforming scholarship into social justice by remaking literary history according to the principles at the very heart of Benjamin's philosophy of history.

Recovering literary texts became a way to "seize hold of a memory as it flashes up at a moment of danger."[4] The danger it redressed was the risk and consequences of exclusion. The desire for a full record, one whose completeness is defined by its multiplicity of voice, drives recovery. Perhaps the epitome of this movement is the *Heath Anthology of American Literature*, whose version of literary history offers itself as a testament to the plurality of the nation.[5] Projects like the *Heath Anthology* have added not just pages to our literary history but also a consciousness of how essential all these voices are, precisely because they can never be unified as voices. Instead, like the cultural messages they impart, they have a unity of function rather than object. Benjamin would say that we recover texts to redeem ourselves. Thus scholars working in the civil rights era restored the slave experience to the record, while feminists successfully reconfigured women's literature as a crucial part of literary history and canonical literature. In 2011 a range of publications and media events across the country celebrated Harriet Beecher Stowe's two hundredth birthday, a recognition that directly resulted from decades of recovery work, which has also played a role in changing notions of the archive and its place in (literary) history.

The focal material of the preceding chapters has constructed a rather unusual archive, one whose composition has been as much a subject of this book as its particular examples, each of which has been undergirded by questions regarding the nature and condition of the archive as it functions in the construction of literary history. Though much of this discussion has focused on the archive's past, it has significant bearing on the archive to come. In his work on the Holocaust, Giorgio Agamben defines the archive as "a system of relations between the unsaid and the said."[6] We might reconfigure Agamben's definition for today by describing the archive as a system of relations between the offline and the digital. In the offline archive, fingerprints, smudges, erasures, and pen pressure invite readers to consider the residue of writing in human terms, suggesting a scene of writing that supplies the researcher with points of contact with the author.[7] As we discovered in reordering and reassembling Jane Johnston Schoolcraft's oeuvre, patching together the remnants of authorship in Truth and Chesnut, relocating Bond's novel in literary history, and reassessing *Macaria*'s double-sided publication history, the authorial body lurks somewhere among the detritus that the archive comprises. The act of preservation that composes the archive also preserves poststructuralism's forbidden subject: authorial intention as a feature of literary production and scholarly activity.

Perhaps the first important step in understanding what the past of book history and the future of media studies have in common is to think of the archive in two distinct ways: as a condition, and in terms of the processes it encourages in users.[8] As a condition, the archive locates and preserves the past. However disordered it may be, an offline archive is managed by librarians or curators who preserve, verify factual information about, and keep careful records of its content, which is usually historical in nature. Of course, even these most minimal structures always already figure as an act of interpretation—it would be naïve, not to mention alarmingly un-Foucauldian, to think otherwise—but there can nevertheless be a certain randomness to the offline archive. The digital archive, in contrast, is prepared and managed by an editor, who often has a scholarly stake in the material.[9] No matter how carefully editors of digital archives work to preserve the random delights and intellectual freedom of discovery, the researcher in the online archive encounters editing as a necessary condition that inevitably becomes a naturalized invisible context.

Yet the offline archive also has its liabilities, which are perhaps even more invisible. When researchers turn to the archive to assemble materials and ephemera in hopes of discovering new evidence, we encourage what Agamben terms "a vicarious past" that we take pleasure in creating.[10] The offline archive permits us to use our imagination in ways not typically associated with scholarship—or scholars, for that matter. As we come into contact with the scene of writing, we become eyewitnesses and reconstructors, even as we maintain our status as deconstructors. The materiality of the offline archive fosters our delusions of objectivity while encouraging us to breach the bounds between past and present with our own fantasies.

As the preceding chapters have come to grips with some of the disparities between historicism and historical materialism, they have also clarified why the history of the book is so well suited for unpacking contemporary concerns about materiality brought on by the emergent technologies of digital culture. For one thing, historians of the book have called attention to a more complex notion of the material. Text made manifest in printed form embodies the nature of materiality, and historians of the book have crucially understood that "materiality is always something more than 'mere' matter: an excess, force, vitality, relationality, or difference that renders matter active, self-creative, productive, unpredictable."[11] The earliest studies of the book compelled us to think of the relationship between print and culture as powerful, transformative, and unpredictable. Studies of print culture are, after all, studies of the most extensive archive of human culture.

The digital archive is no less an archive of human culture, and, crucially, it is no less mediated than other forms. By virtue of its constructedness, the digital archive is far less a product of the post-human than it is a reflection of the post-Cartesian understanding of the material as such. Although it appears to preclude the haphazard human element, it discloses a degree of intentionality regarding its subject and editorial principles. But I don't want simply to aver or even examine the static versus dynamic manipulation of information associated with the broadest distinctions between online and offline archives. Indeed, some of the most sophisticated digital interfaces—the light box feature of the Dickinson archive or the Collex software available through NINES—prompt us to revisit how the relationship between subject and scholar constructs a hidden authorial presence. As we become more and more adept at manipulating digital content so as to, as the Collex website puts it, "collect, annotate, and tag online objects" and "repurpose" text, we posit authorship as a shared—and historical—position. Online, the person who authorizes ephemera by incorporating it into a collection of authorial remains takes on a new but familiar role, facing some of the same issues visible in the offline construction and publication of Hannah Bond's novel and Mary Chesnut's diary. These case studies remind us to attend—with added caution—to how the relationships between subject and scholar merge, intervene in, and shape the archive, disclosing a shifting conception of intentionality for that archive's gatekeeper, subject, and user.

Thus, rather than composing a screed against the digital archive, which in severing information from its mediated form turns us regrettably post-human, I instead take up N. Katherine Hayles's insight that "when narrative functionalities change, a new kind of reader is produced by the text."[12] In light of recent thinking about the composition of the online archive, we might say that digital archives also produce a new kind of author, who becomes historically and conceptually a co-author or kind of postmodern biographer.[13] We can also see, just as sharply, the ways in which the offline archive retains—to a dangerous degree—an air of primacy and even privacy, enabling the scholar to select and represent materials according to terms we call argument but an editor would call principles of selection. What we do not talk about is the way physical and textual material can generate the kind of creative processes that many think of as the domain of the artist, whether visual or literary.

Returning now to this book's key terms, I want to elaborate the linkages between (re)mediation, memory, history, testimony, and loss, and the case studies I have used to explore them. The online archive calls attention to the degree of mediation in the production of the archive. The terms of that mediation—to which the work of Robert Darnton and Jerome McGann, among others, has sensitized us—seem straightforward. The archive's principle of selection is embedded in an argument figured by the order and presentation of its materials. Yet we do not take into consideration the function of artifice when we interpret the scrap of paper or random photograph as we would (and do) when, say, Whitman, in *Specimen Days*, emphasizes the authenticity of his words by telling us that they are pencil scratchings taken from bloodstained notebooks.[14] Though we are apt to struggle with making solid distinctions between memory and history in our own work, we tend to treat ephemera like the supposedly definitive testimony of an expert witness. In the end, I wonder if we have turned to ephemera as a stay against the loss of other scholarly articles of faith: authority, intentionality, and perhaps even, as in the Pulitzer Prize–winning *Mary Chesnut's Civil War*, narrative itself.

Is recovery over? Not yet. It has just taken a new form. Digitization projects are the recovery work of our age. In the context of this discussion, it is notable how clearly these acts of recovery strike a chord of loss: loss of paper, loss of the book, even the end of narrative. Earlier arguments against recovery also bemoaned the loss it provoked: of history, literature, aesthetic value, even culture itself.[15] Today, ironically, noncanonical and newly recovered texts and authors feel the threat of loss most keenly. Though the Internet promises to expand access, digitization projects require funding, resources are scarce, and already canonized texts and authors tend to take precedence.[16]

One purpose of the foregoing chapters has been to explore, in depth, the history of concerns about the archive, broadly speaking, as they played out in the nineteenth century. Schoolcraft's archive revealed the struggle for authority along the lines of literacy. Exploring how literacy works in a multilingual, multicultural context exposed the archive's palimpsestuous nature. As with the work of all the authors considered here, carefully peeling back the layers of composition, revision, publication, and circulation reveals distinct registers, each tuned to a different purpose. Schoolcraft used literacy to remediate the damage done to her and her people. A poem like "To my ever beloved & lamented Son William Henry" might once have been dismissed as cliché, but here appears as a complex collision of the expectations Schoolcraft faced as a mother, a writer, and an Ojibwe. Though the poem lacks textual ties to her Ojibwe roots, her refusal to reprint it honors her cultural ties. Her use of Margaret Taylor's "My Mother" anticipates the mashup world of Web 2.0, in which repurposing grants new and unexpected meanings, and successful mashups reflect the ultraliteracy of a culture so inundated with itself that pastiche and self-parody are its most popular expressions.

Sojourner Truth manipulated the protocols of authorship, interleaving word and image to expose what Matthew Kirschenbaum has called "the dialects of materiality."[17] Her excursions into the world of print push its literal and figurative boundaries. Resisting literacy herself, Truth makes a radical statement about power, ownership, and agency by assembling other people's words, images, and even signatures to create the composite entity that we recognize today as Sojourner Truth. In putting together the 1875 edition of her narrative, Truth also anticipated the principles of the mashup, using the ethos of crowd sourcing: she personally selected and ordered the material included in her "Book of Life" from Stowe's "Libyan Sybil" in those signatures, which literally and figuratively pressed into service the hands of other luminaries to shine a light on her own status as a historical personage, utilizing new technologies of reproduction that presaged the end of handwriting's dominance. We can picture Truth, were she alive today, as the popular blogger whose Web presence both confers and accumulates power.

Like oral cultures, participatory cultures, which measure value by utility, have a different slant on originality.[18] A blog's quality is measured by active engagement, that is, by the number of posts it generates rather than the number of hits it receives. Authority resonates with public culture rather than dictating or dominating it. Those who don't code in HTML might seem only to replicate and amend, edit and customize, producing resolutely derivative texts. We have become like Sojourner Truth: compositors, not composers, layering content and amalgamating forms rather than initializing or authoring. Truth was our progenitor, successfully converting the viewers of the image she carefully composed into true believers.

Hannah Bond's rejection of publication approaches literary history from its void. Her unpublished novel calls attention to the rigorous codes that control our knowledge of the past and its productions. Of all the authors' works discussed here, the history of her text bears the least resemblance to anything in contemporary open access online publication. Though boutique forms of digital information production such as blogging derive from the same impulse to publish as more conventional print outlets, they are not vetted by gatekeepers according to principles of originality, authorship, and legitimacy. Were Bond herself to publish today, she would not have needed to reveal her identity or submit herself to the judgments of a New York editor. Rather, she could have published online, under any name she wanted, and both her amalgamating style and her online identity would have been embraced by our mashup culture. She could have been both a storyteller and a storyseller, along the lines of Amanda Hocking, who made $2 million self-publishing e-books before garnering a $2 million book deal with St. Martin's Press. Readers, rather than a publisher, conferred her success. According to the *New York Times*, "she has become—along with the likes of Nora Roberts, James Patterson and Stieg Larsson—one of the best-selling e-authors on Amazon. In that time, she has grossed approximately $2 million. . . . 'She's just a really good storyteller,' [her editor at St. Martin's Press, Rose] Hilliard says. 'Whatever that thing is that makes you want to stay up late at night to read one more chapter—she has it.'"[19] While we will never know if Hannah Bond could have competed with the likes of Amanda Hocking, different publication protocols would have given her a fair try at doing so.

Macaria's Möbius strip–like publication history upsets the traditional primacy of the first edition and its place in scholarly study, making way for a larger discussion about the function of multiple editions in understanding literary history. The novel was published on both sides of the Mason-Dixon line, but its publication dates were complicated by sectional differences; these regional differences create the half twist characteristic of the Möbius strip. Paradoxically, neither and both the Northern and Southern editions are "firsts." We must study them both, simultaneously. Despite the textual adaptations made in consideration of regional reader demographics—such as the removal of the dedication to the Confederate troops in the New York edition—the novel's ongoing popularity in both North and South invites us to reconsider the value of editions as a gauge of cultural history.

The theoretical insights provided by *Macaria*'s publication history increase exponentially when we turn to the many iterations of Mary Chesnut's Diary, which changed considerably as it was published and republished over time. Unlike *Macaria*, which remained relatively stable through its various editions, Chesnut's text expanded in size and editorial complexity. From Avary and Martin's decidedly pro-South 1905 version, which they wanted to call "With the Heroes of Dixie," to Ben Ames Williams's mythologizing 1949 *Diary from Dixie*, to C. Vann Woodward's Pulitzer Prize–winning *Mary Chesnut's Civil War*, each edition bears indelible traces of its editors. Because these editions bear little resemblance to one another, they require more than an outsized variorum analysis. Rather, to leverage the collective power of the key terms proposed by *Thinking Outside the Book*, we must consider all of these iterations as both autonomous entities and mutually constitutive ersatz texts, perpetually recovering a text that will never be all there, in part because of Chesnut's radical refusal to conform to generic standards. Pledging its allegiance to no single genre allows the diary to belong to all genres.

Walter Benjamin provides a framework that allows us to make sense of these reverberating texts and the work entailed in understanding their histories. He reminds us that a fact becomes "historical posthumously, as it were, through events that may be separated from it by thousands of years." In this light, "a historian who takes this as his point of departure stops telling the sequence of events like the beads of a rosary. Instead, he grasps the constellation that his own era has formed with a definite earlier one. Thus he establishes a conception of the present as the 'time of the now' which is shot through with chips of Messianic time."[20] This book has shown how the digital culture "of the now" is "shot through" with publication purposes and practices of the past. Rather than seeing the present as definitive loss—or gain—we must remember that "in every era the attempt must be made anew to wrest tradition away from a conformism that is about to overpower it. . . . Only that historian will have the gift of fanning the spark of hope in the past who is firmly convinced that even the dead will not be safe from the enemy if he wins. And this enemy has not ceased to be victorious."[21] But where, according to the redeeming nature of recovery, the enemy was once *ex*clusion, the threat posed by the digitization of everything is *in*clusion.[22] Few would argue for a return to the exclusivity that guided earlier models of literary history. Yet all of us must now contend with the overwhelming availability of text—the data and metadata of our world—and think outside the book.

Notes

Introduction

1. Henry Jenkins et al., *Confronting the Challenges ofa Participatory Culture: Media Education for the 21st Century* (Cambridge: MIT Press, 2009), xi, citing Amanda Lenhart and Mary Madden, "Teen Content Creators and Consumers," Pew Internet & American Life Project, November 2, 2005, www.pewinternet.org.
2. In the face of the enormous prominence of the book as "the" signifier of cultural significance, I join many others in adopting the broadest possible construction of the term. See, for instance, the mission statement of the Institute for the History of the Book: "We use the word 'book' broadly, even metaphorically, to talk about what has come before—and what might come next" (www.futureofthebook.org). The capaciousness of the form (and the term) has given rise to a move in the field away from "book history" toward "print culture." For a succinct exposition of the theory underpinning this development in the field, see Carla Hesse, "Books in Time," in *The Future of the Book*, ed. Geoffrey Nunberg (Berkeley: University of California Press, 1996), 21–36.
3. Jenkins et al., *Confronting the Challenges*, xiii.
4. Ibid., 8.
5. This book joins others that look to the synergies between the past and our contemporary context. Especially helpful to me in thinking about these resonances, though from a different continent, was Andrew Piper's *Dreaming in Books* (Chicago: University of Chicago Press, 2009).
6. I have taken the term "parallax" and its conceptual value from Paul Giles's *Remapping American Literature* (New York: Oxford University Press, 2011). For the purposes of

his study, the notion helps Giles name the function of comparison for the writers and thinkers he discusses. The series of radical contrasts and juxtapositions of both time and space help Giles do more than simply reveal important connections; they also aid him in positing a theory of history. Thus, in a return to modes of authorship that had fewer ties to the stable—because located—structures of cultural production, our Internet-enabled world more closely resembles revolutionary France than it does twentieth-century publication practices. As Hesse explains: "Legal and institutional changes aimed at ensuring the dominance of the book—a cultural form that encouraged slow, reasoned reflections on events rather than the spontaneous and rapid interventions made possible by newspaper and pamphlet production. The author of the book, who had property rights in his or her work, could therefore be held legally accountable for what he or she published." Hesse, "Books in Time," 26.

7. Roger Whitson, "Digital Blake 2.0," in *Blake 2.0: William Blake in Twentieth-Century Art, Music, and Culture*, ed. Steve Clark, Tristanne Connolly, and Jason Whittaker (New York: Palgrave, 2012), 41–55, has helped me think about the distinct questions and problems that digital texts and archives provoke. Whitson's work usefully challenges us to conceptualize and thereby capitalize on the unique differences a Web-based text or archive has to offer.
8. Here I am extending—backward—Carla Hesse's insight on digital culture: "Digitization . . . has created a new terrain that reconceives our mental landscape (both forms of knowledge and modes of apprehension and exchange) in performative rather than structural terms." Hesse, "Books in Time," 32.
9. Kathleen Fitzpatrick, *Planned Obsolescence* (New York: New York University Press, 2011).
10. The field of book history has moved from a focus on things bibliographic to those more broadly rhetorical. Bibliographers became book historians, who, in turn, have moved toward ever-broadening formations of the field such as print culture, media studies, and communications. See, for instance, John Durham Peters's expansive study of this history in *Speaking into the Air: A History of the Idea of Communication* (Chicago: University of Chicago Press, 1999).
11. I have taken this phrase from Andy Clark's *Natural-Born Cyborgs: Minds, Technologies, and the Future of Human Intelligence* (New York: Oxford University Press, 2003), 60.
12. Carla Hesse observes, "Most striking to the historian, in witnessing the remaking of the literary system in the present age, is the almost unwitting impulse to reconceptualize the key institutions of modern literary culture—the book, the author, the reader and the library in terms of time, motion, and modes of action, rather than in terms of space, objects, and actors." Hesse, "Books in Time," 32. Though my set of terms differs slightly from Hesse's, her description of the switch from space to time places a useful emphasis on the active power of the terminology rather than as a static formation.
13. Elizabeth Grosz, *The Nick of Time: Politics, Evolution, and the Untimely* (Durham: Duke University Press, 2004), 21.
14. Jenkins et al., *Confronting the Challenges*, 8.
15. This book would not have been possible without a slew of texts written by Nina Baym: *Woman's Fiction* (Ithaca: Cornell University Press, 1978); *Feminism and*

American Literary History (New Brunswick: Rutgers University Press, 1992); *American Women Writers and the Work of History* (New Brunswick: Rutgers University Press, 1995); and *American Women of Letters and the Nineteenth-Century Sciences* (New Brunswick: Rutgers University Press, 2004).

16. Anthony Grafton, *The Footnote: A Curious History* (Cambridge: Harvard University Press, 1999); Patricia Meyer Spacks, *Gossip* (Chicago: University of Chicago Press, 1986).
17. The history of how women writers rose to a position of dominance is rendered with awesome clarity by Susan S. Williams in *Reclaiming Authorship: Literary Women in America, 1850–1900* (Philadelphia: University of Pennsylvania Press, 2006).
18. Piper, *Dreaming in Books;* Fitzpatrick, *Planned Obsolescence.*
19. Even one of the most prescient of these publications, Meredith McGill's *American Literature and the Culture of Reprinting, 1834–1853* (Philadelphia: University of Pennsylvania Press, 2006), relies on publication as its primary qualification.
20. Here my experimental methodology has been influenced by Franco Moretti's *Graphs, Maps, Trees: Abstract Models for a Literary History* (New York: Verso, 2005).
21. Robert Darnton, "What Is the History of Books?," *Daedalus* 111.3 (1982): 65–83; Jerome McGann, *Radiant Textuality: Literature after the World Wide Web* (New York: Palgrave, 2004.)
22. William Charvat devotes a chapter of *The Profession of Authorship in America, 1800–1870*, ed. Matthew Bruccoli (New York: Columbia University Press, 1992), to the way Longfellow and his publishers exploited multiple formats in order to expand his command of the market (106–55). Oren Bracha describes the publisher Putnam and Co. releasing Washington Irving's works in 1854 in a variety of formats—paper, hardbound, calf, and morocco—the only difference between these volumes being the material from which the book's cover was made. Oren Bracha, "The Ideology of Authorship Revisited: Authors, Markets, and Liberal Values in Early American Copyright," *Yale Law Journal* 118.2 (November 2008): 239, available at www.yalelawjournal.org.
23. According to Leah Price, "reading is only one among many uses to which printed matter can be put." Leah Price, "From the History of a Book to a 'History of the Book,'" *Representations* 108 (2009): 120–38. She further explores this subject in delightful depth in *How to Do Things with Books in Victorian England* (Princeton: Princeton University Press, 2012). To these discussions I would add that publication is only one among many forms a book can take. For an exemplary discussion of the abstract and changing forms of a "book," see Matthew Kirschenbaum's discussion of William Gibson's *Agrippa* in *Mechanisms* (Cambridge: MIT Press, 2009), 1–25, 213–39. A broad range of other literary scholars have since joined Price in examining the ways in which books, literal, figurative, and material, have moved to the center of our analyses from the margins of history.
24. Among those to approach this subject in recent years—albeit from its margins—is David Shields in *Reality Hunger: A Manifesto* (New York: Knopf, 2010).
25. Henry Jenkins's important *Convergence Culture: Where Old and New Media Collide* (New York: New York University Press, 2006) has been essential in developing my thinking about navigating the gap between my field of study and contemporary culture.

26. From the pages of the *New York Times* to the shelves of academic libraries, scholars, cultural critics, and lay readers are linked in their shared anxiety over the future—or lack thereof—the book. Yet as Paul Duguid notes in "Material Matters: The Past and Futurology of the Book," in *The Book History Reader*, ed. David Finkelstein and Alistair McCleery (London: Routledge, 2002), "futurologists do have a habit of announcing both deaths and births prematurely" (494). See also the more recent collection of Robert Darnton's work, *The Case for Books* (New York: Public Affairs, 2009).
27. I have cited the MacArthur commission's study on education for the twenty-first century. The studies that have taken up this question are too numerous to cite here but should include Cathy Davidson, *Now You See It: How the Brain Science of Attention Will Transform How We Live, Work, and Learn* (New York: Viking, 2011); as well as Siva Vaidhyanathan, *The Googlization of Everything (And Why We Should Worry)* (Berkeley: University of California Press, 2011).

1. (Re)Mediation (Literacy Rethought)

1. This virtual museum exhibit dedicated to the preservation and extension of Ojibwe culture joins a handful of other forays into the digital world, including a companion site to a Native American anthology edited by Siobhan Senier, at https://indnewengland.omeka.net.
2. Timothy B. Powell and Larry P. Aitken, *chi-ayy ya agg* (Wisdom Keeper), "Building a Digital Archive Based on Traditional Ojibwe Teachings," in *The American Literature Scholar in the Digital Age*, ed. Amy E. Earhart and Andrew Jewell (Ann Arbor: University of Michigan Press, 2010), 252. The spelling of "Ojibwe" varies; I use "Ojibwe" here, in keeping with Powell and Aitken's spelling, unless I am quoting or referring to a published text that uses a different variant.
3. Ibid., 253.
4. Ibid., 251.
5. Ibid., 253.
6. In Emerson, the power of speech shapes his style, his rhetorical figures. In Schoolcraft, her moves are freighted—indeed, motivated—by the distance created by her status as a mixed-race Ojibwe woman. As R. Jackson Wilson observes, "Emerson would write, but he would not exactly fit the recently discovered cultural category of 'author.'" Wilson goes on to explore—and many others have followed in his wake—the formative pressure of the lecture circuit not just on Emerson's style but on his very thought. He sums it up neatly: "Ralph Waldo Emerson was not 'Man Thinking' but 'Man Saying.'" R. Jackson Wilson, "Emerson as Lecturer: Man Thinking, Man Saying," in *The Cambridge Companion to Ralph Waldo Emerson*, ed. Joel Porte and Saundra Morris (Cambridge: Cambridge University Press, 1999), 77.
7. Here I am pursuing A. LaVonne Brown Rouff's insight that Schoolcraft's work uses "multiple-voiced discourse." A. LaVonne Brown Rouff, "Early Native American Women Authors: Jane Johnston Schoolcraft, Sarah Winnemucca, Alice Callahan, E. Pauline Johnson, and Zirkala-Sa," in *Native American Women's Writing, c. 1800–1924: An Anthology*, ed. Karen L. Kilcup (Oxford: Blackwell, 1998), 81.

8. Robert Dale Parker, *The Invention of Native American Literature* (Ithaca: Cornell University Press, 2003), which repositions Native American writing within the oral/poetic traditions it values, has helped me rethink the place of publication and literacy under examination here.
9. See Leon Jackson, *The Business of Letters: Authorial Economies in Antebellum America* (Stanford: Stanford University Press, 2008), esp. chap. 3, "Authorship and Gift Exchange." For a discussion of the tradition of scribal publication dating back to seventeenth-century New England, see David Hall, "Not in Print yet Published," chap. 2 in *Ways of Writing* (Philadelphia: University of Pennsylvania Press, 2008).
10. In Laura Mielke's study of *The Literary Voyager* in relation to the Schoolcrafts, "'Sorrow in excess!' The Limits of Sympathy in the Ethnography of George Catlin, Jane Johnston Schoolcraft, and Henry Rowe Schoolcraft," chap. 6 in *Moving Encounters: Sympathy and the Indian Question in Antebellum Literature* (Amherst: University of Massachusetts Press, 2008), it is figured as "a family activity" (139). Her treatment of the magazine emphasizes its use of "moving encounters" to "proclaim affective understanding of American Indians and calling for reader sympathy" (116).
11. Louise Erdrich, *Books and Islands in Ojibwa Country* (Washington, D.C.: National Geographic, 2003), 5.
12. I also consulted John D. Nichols and Earl Nyholm, eds., *The Concise Dictionary of Minnesota Ojibwe* (Minneapolis: University of Minnesota Press, 1995).
13. Arnold Krupat, "America's Histories," *American Literary History* 10.1 (Spring 1998): 124.
14. As Renee Bergland cautions, "situating Native America and Native Americans in the nineteenth century risks displacing them from their present." Renee Bergland, "Afterword," *ESQ: A Journal of the American Renaissance* 52.1–2 (2006): 141.
15. Jane Johnston Schoolcraft, *The Sound the Stars Make Rushing through the Sky: The Writings of Jane Johnston Schoolcraft*, ed. Robert Dale Parker (Philadelphia: University of Pennsylvania Press, 2007). Subsequent quotations from this edition are cited parenthetically in the text as *Writings*. In addition to Walter Ong's influential *Orality and Literacy* (New York: Methuen, 1982), the work of Ruth Finnegan as well as that of John Durham Peters has moved the study of oral culture forward.
16. Here we could also consider the notes that often either introduced or followed the tales written by Henry Schoolcraft.
17. In both the fourth and fifth editions, *The Heath Anthology* reprints two of Schoolcraft's tales.
18. In her field-defining study of oral poetry, Ruth Finnegan finds that "Composition," "Transmission," and "Performance" are the three characteristics that need to be present for a work to be considered "oral," even when transcribed. For Finnegan, the most essential of these three to the integrity of a definition of "oral poetry" is performance: the precondition for poetry to be considered oral. Ruth Finnegan, *Oral Poetry: Its Nature, Significance, and Social Context* (Bloomington: Indiana University Press, 1992), 13–28.
19. These features of the oral tale have prompted Michelle Fankhauser to treat the oral tale as a "paratextual" element of the published tale; see "Booked: Womanhood Is Too Tightly Bound to Give Me Scope" (Ph.D. diss., Washington State University, 2010), chap. 1.

20. See Parker's introduction in Schoolcraft, *Writings*, 1–73. As Parker observes, we must use the tales "to challenge Euroamerican ideas of authorship" (54).
21. Renee Bergland, author of *National Uncanny: Indian Ghosts and American Subjects* (Hanover: University Press of New England, 2000), a pioneering study of the importance and impact of American Indian culture on emerging Anglo-American forms of literary culture, presented an earlier version of this chapter on my behalf at a 2006 conference. Reporting back on its reception, she remarked on how difficult it was to sound out the parts of the paper that quoted the transliterated Ojibwe.
23. For a detailed discussion of the refrain as a forgotten but culturally resonant poetic device, see Max Cavitch, "Stephen Crane's Poetic Refrain," in "Poetry," special issue, *ESQ: A Journal of the American Renaissance* 54.1–4 (2008): 33–54.
24. Eliza Richards, *Gender and the Poetics of Reception in Poe's Circle* (Cambridge: Cambridge University Press, 2004), 4. See also the Poetess Archive, curated by Laura Mandell, http://idhmc.tamu.edu.
25. Henry Schoolcraft used this word to describe his wife's writing; quoted in "An Introduction to the Poetry of Jane Johnston Schoolcraft," appendix 2, in Schoolcraft, *Writings*, 236–39.
26. In a personal e-mail communication, Parker confirmed the typographical details discussed here, as well as the spelling of the pen names, preserved from the original texts.
27. Eliza Richards remains the key source for understanding the complexity of this term; see *Gender and the Poetics of Reception.*
28. Though it focuses on a later period, Gavin Jones, *Strange Talk: The Politics of Dialect Literature in Gilded Age America* (Berkeley: University of California Press, 1999), is an indispensable treatment of dialect in print.
29. Here I am influenced by Bethany Schneider's discussion of this term in her essay "Not for Citation: Jane Johnston Schoolcraft's Synchronic Strategies," in "Poetry," special issue, *ESQ: A Journal of the American Renaissance* 54.1–4 (2008): 111–44. I am also drawing on Eric Gary Anderson, "Indian Agency: Life of Black Hawk and the Counter-colonial Provocations of Early Native American Writing," *ESQ: A Journal of the American Renaissance* 52.1–2 (2006): 75–104, for his insights into how Indian agency "works to de-objectify Indians and challenge this 'inexorable advance" [of white cultural formations], in part by paradoxically setting in motion countercultural transformations whereby Indians themselves mobilize some of the very tools of 'advancement'" (83).
30. Schneider, "Not for Citation," 115.
31. Parker, introduction to Schoolcraft, *Writings*, 73.
32. Ibid., 34. All of my background information on this poem comes from Parker's introduction (34–37).
33. *Literary Voyager*, no. 14, March 28, 1827, in *Schoolcraft's Ojibwa Lodge Stories: Life on Lake Superior*, ed. Philip P. Mason (1962; repr., East Lansing: Michigan State University Press, 1997), 144. Subsequent quotations from *Literary Voyager* are taken from this edition and are cited parenthetically in the text.
34. Parker has identified the source for this poem, indicating that the second line of Schoolcraft's poem quotes Taylor's verbatim (introduction to Schoolcraft, *Writings*, 136). I found Taylor's poem at www.mothers.net, a website that describes

itself as "a virtual community to share the wonders and craft of Motherhood." Quotation are from this source.

35. Letter dated May 11, 1827, in Parker, introduction to *Writings*, 35.
36. Thanks to Barbara Monroe for suggesting I pursue the connection between the unpublished poem and traditional Ojibwe mourning practices.
37. Paul Hackett, "Historical Mourning Practices Observed among the Cree and Ojibwa Indians of the Subartic," *Ethnohistory* 52.3 (Summer 2005): 503–32.
38. For a detailed discussion of Henry Schoolcraft's "free" translation of this poem as evidence of his larger project of cultural dominance, see Schneider, "Not for Citation."
39. In *Punctuation: Art, Politics, and Play* (Durham: Duke University Press, 2008), Jennifer DeVere Brody refers to M. B. Parkes, *Pause and Effect: An Introduction to the History of Punctuation in the West* (Berkeley: University of California Press, 1993), and his understanding that punctuation is purely "a phenomenon of written language" (17).
40. Larry Aitken, in response to the question "How can we remain connected to the old ways?" in the "Ask the Elders" section of the website Gibagadinamaagoom, http://ojibwearchive.sas.upenn.edu (no longer available).
41. Currently the focus on Schoolcraft's work has shifted from her as a scribe of tribal stories to her identity as an author thanks to the work of Karen Kilcup, Robert Dale Parker, LaVonne Brown Ruoff, and Bethany Schneider, among others. Here I refer to Schneider's "Not for Citation."
42. "The medicine text," a term mentioned in Betty Booth Donohue's piece in the MLA volume on teaching nineteenth-century American poetry, was later built into "medicine bundle" by Joshua David Bellin: "The process of interaction and cocreation I name the medicine bundle, a phrase I adapt from its autochthonous sense—sacred objects, bound together for ritual or ceremonial purposes—to designate the complex, conflictual, cross-cultural acts that lie at the heart of American life and literature." Joshua David Bellin, *Medicine Bundle* (Philadelphia: University of Pennsylvania Press, 2007), 4.
43. Ibid., 13.
44. Lisa Gitelman, "Epilogue," in *Always Already New* (Cambridge: MIT Press, 2008), 155.
45. See Virginia Jackson, *Dickinson's Misery: A Theory of Lyric Reading* (Princeton: Princeton University Press, 2005), for an invigorating look at the expectations and associations genre created in readers of the published Dickinson as a "lyric" poet.

2. Memory (Authorship Revisited)

1. Theodore Parker, "The American Scholar," in *Works of Theodore Parker*, ed. George Willis Cooke (Boston: American Unitarian Association, 1907), 37.
2. Walter Ong, in *Orality and Literacy* (New York: Methuen, 1982), addresses the "persistent tendency, even among scholars, to think of writing as the basic form of language" (5), and it is this tendency that has kept scholars from appreciating—and understanding—the important work that speech and image does for Sojourner Truth.

3. Frances Dana Gage's description is most frequently cited. Harriet Beecher Stowe also includes the turban in her article "The Libyan Sibyl," *Atlantic Monthly*, April 1863, 473–82.
4. My thinking on this subject has been helped by Stacey Margolis, *The Public Life of Privacy in Nineteenth-Century American Literature* (Durham: Duke University Press, 2005).
5. Nell Irvin Painter discusses Truth's commitment to orality in terms of her perfectionism in *Sojourner Truth: A Life, a Symbol* (New York: Norton, 1996), 38.
6. According to research Ong discusses at length, "writing has to be personally interiorized to affect thinking processes." Ong, *Orality and Literacy*, 56. Thus, although Truth had contact with literacy and even utilized many of its formations, she retained her independence from it by remaining illiterate. For further discussion of Ong's broader claim that writing restructures consciousness, see ibid., 77–114.
7. Sojourner Truth, *Narrative of Sojourner Truth* (Boston: Yarrington and Sons, 1850), 109.
8. Ibid., 45.
9. In "Speech, Writing, Code: Three Worldviews," in *My Mother Was a Computer: Digital Subjects and Literary Texts* (Chicago: University of Chicago Press, 2005), 39–62, N. Katherine Hayles takes a systematic approach to appraising these three forms and their conceptual frameworks in order to work through the areas of overlap and autonomy between them. I have appended image to her discussion.
10. Truth, *Narrative* (1850 ed.), xii.
11. See Jean Baudrillard, *Simulacra and Simulation*, trans. Sheila Faria Glaser (Ann Arbor: University of Michigan Press, 1994).
12. Refuting this assertion, Truth remarked: "There is one place where she speaks of me as coming from Africa. My grandmother and my husband's mother came from Africa, but I did not." "Letter from Sojourner Truth," *Boston Commonwealth*, July 3, 1863, quoted in Painter, *Sojourner Truth*, 163. In correcting these errors, she de facto corrects the central error of the piece: that Truth is dead.
13. Harriet Beecher Stowe, "The Libyan Sibyl," reprinted in *Narrative of Sojourner Truth* (1884 ed.), ed. Nell Irvin Painter (New York: Penguin, 1998), 103–17.
14. Ibid., 114–15.
15. Ibid., 115.
16. In her chapter on Sojourner Truth, Jeannine DeLombard makes important use of what she calls "the testimonial posture that authorized formerly enslaved African Americans' contributions to the debate over the South's peculiar institution." Jeannine Marie DeLombard, "Precarious Evidence: Sojourner Truth and the Mathias Scandal," in *Slavery on Trial: Law, Abolitionism, and Print Culture* (Chapel Hill: University of North Carolina Press, 2007), 71.
17. Gage's transcription of the speech appeared in the *New York Independent*, April 23, 1863.
18. Scholars have come to this conclusion on the basis of a comparison with an earlier version of the speech published June 21, 1851, in the *Anti-Slavery Bugle*, transcribed by Marius Robinson. For the sake of comparison, I reprint the earlier version here: "'May I say a few words?' Receiving an affirmative answer, she proceeded; 'I want to say a few words about this matter. I am a woman's rights.

I have as much muscle as any man, and can do as much work as any man. I have plowed and reaped and husked and chopped and mowed, and can any man do more than that? I have heard much about the sexes being equal; I can carry as much as any man, and can eat as much too, if I can get it. I am as strong as any man that is now. As for intellect, all I can say is, if woman have a pint full and a man a quart—why can't she have her little pint full? You need not be afraid to give us our rights for fear we will take too much, for we can't take more than our pint'll hold. The poor men seem to be all in confusion, and don't know what to do. Why children, if you have woman's rights give it to her and you'll feel better. You will have your own rights, and they won't be so much trouble. I can't read, but I can hear. I have heard the bible and have learned that Eve caused man to sin. Well if woman upset the world, do give her a chance to set it right side up again. The Lady has spoken about Jesus, how he never spurned woman from him, and she was right. When Lazarus died, Mary and Martha came to him with faith and love and besought him to raise their brother. And Jesus wept—and Lazarus came forth. And how came Jesus into the world? Through God who created him and woman who bore him. Man, where is your part? But the women are coming up, blessed be God, and a few of the men are coming with them. But man is in a tight place, the poor slave is on him, woman is coming on him, and he is surely between a hawk and a buzzard.'"

19. Henry Jenkins, Sam Ford, and Joshua Green, *Spreadable Media: Creating Value and Meaning in a Networked Culture* (New York: New York University Press, 2013).
20. After her death, the image was used by her tireless supporter and promoter Frances Titus to raise money for the Sojourner Truth memorial that was eventually erected in Florence, Massachusetts. See Kathleen Collins, "Shadow and Substance: Sojourner Truth," *History of Photography* 7.3 (July–September 1983): 194.
21. Painter, *Sojourner Truth*, 139.
22. Collins, "Shadow and Substance," 195.
23. Roland Barthes, *Camera Lucida*, trans. Richard Howard (New York: Hill and Wang, 1981), 76.
24. Collins uses the copyright notice to help date the various photographs of Sojourner Truth. Those that do not bear the copyright stamp are believed to have been taken prior to 1864. Collins, "Shadow and Substance," 189–90.
25. Andrea Volpe, "Collecting the Nation: Visions of Nationalism in Two Civil War–Era Photograph Albums," in *Acts of Possession: Collecting in America*, ed. Leah Dilworth (New Brunswick: Rutgers University Press, 2003), 89–162.
26. I am glossing Barthes here: "Painting can feign reality without having seen it. . . . [I]n Photography I can never deny that the thing has been there" (*Camera Lucida*, 76).
27. Nell Painter explains in her notes to the Penguin edition: "During the years when Truth dressed as a farm worker, photography had not yet been invented, and she was too obscure to rate a painted portrait. By the time photography was invented in England and France in 1839, Truth was over forty and living in New York City." Truth, *Narrative* (1884 ed.), 253n76.
28. Sonja Neef reviews the historical association of handwriting as a physical embodiment of the writer in "Authentic Events: The Diaries of Anne Frank and the Alleged Diaries of Adolf Hitler," in *Sign Here! Handwriting in the Age of New*

Media, ed. Sonja Neef, José van Dijck, and Eric Ketelaar (Amsterdam: Amsterdam University Press, 2006), 23–50.

29. Anna Chen, "In One's Own Hand: Seeing Manuscripts in a Digital Age," *Digital Humanities Quarterly* 6.2 (2012): 6.
30. Sonja Neef and José van Dijck, *Sign Here!* quoted ibid., 24.
31. Truth, *Narrative* (1850 ed.), 187.
32. Painter, *Sojourner Truth*, 261.
33. Unlike DeLombard, I see Truth deliberately trading on "the cultural anxieties about the credibility of black speech." DeLombard, "Precarious Evidence," 98.
34. Truth, *Narrative* (1875 ed.), quoted in Jean Fagan Yellin, *Women and Sisters: The Antislavery Feminists in American Culture* (New Haven: Yale University Press, 1989), 77.
35. There were other sacrifices as well. For instance, by adapting her message to the market for slave narratives, she sometimes muffled her evangelical message under the noises of authorship. Yet we should also consider the ending Truth and Gilbert chose for the *Narrative*, an homage to her former master for coming to see that slavery was evil. This decidedly evangelical ending stresses the saving of his soul over the condemnation of slavery and its practitioners. See Painter, *Sojourner Truth*, 110.
36. The photographs that James commissioned Alvin Langdon Coburn to take for the New York Edition (1907–1909) demonstrate James's refusal of the overly particularized quotidian detail of early realism. Jonathan Freedman analyzes how James incorporated photography not for its indexical capacity—to establish and document the real—but rather for its ability to represent iconically. See Jonathan Freedman, "Henry James, the Novel, and the Mediascapes of Modernity," in *The Oxford History of the Novel in English*, vol. 6: *The American Novel, 1870–1940*, ed. Priscilla Wald and Michael A. Elliott (Oxford: Oxford University Press, 2014), 234–54.

3. History (Publication Redefined)

1. "Professor Says He Has Solved a Mystery over a Slave's Novel," *New York Times*, September 19, 2013.
2. Michel Foucault, *Language, Counter-Memory, Practice*, ed. Donald F. Bouchard (Ithaca: Cornell University Press, 1977); Stanley Fish, *Is There a Text in This Class? The Authority of Interpretive Communities* (Cambridge: Harvard University Press, 1982). John Bryant, *The Fluid Text: A Theory of Revision and Editing for Book and Screen* (Ann Arbor: University of Michigan Press, 2002), has been enormously helpful to me in redefining the notions of text and publication.
3. Henry Louis Gates Jr., introduction to *The Bondwoman's Narrative by Hannah Crafts* (New York: Time Warner Books, 2002), xxx.
4. Ibid., xxxi.
5. Harriet Wilson, *Our Nig, or, Sketches from the life of a free Black* (Boston: Rand and Avery, 1859).
6. In *Slavery on Trial: Law, Abolitionism, and Print Culture* (Chapel Hill: University of North Carolina Press, 2007), Jeannine Marie DeLombard adds to our

understanding of print forms available to African Americans by exploring the legal brief as an important form of self-expression for African Americans working against laws prohibiting their freedom.

7. Genre expectations were not nearly as rigid when it came to writers on the other side of the color line. White authors such as Harriet Beecher Stowe and Mary Henderson Eastman might make fact fiction when it came to racial subject matter, but the reverse was not a possibility, as the example of the African American James Williams shows. In 1838, on publishing what ultimately turned out to be a fictional autobiography, Williams was branded a liar for using the fiction form rather than sticking with the factual narrative open to black writers at the time. In fact, *The Authentic Narrative of James Williams, an American Slave* (New York: American Anti-Slavery Society, 1838) isn't "authentic" at all. Though "dictated" to the abolitionist and poet John Greenleaf Whittier, it's a novel. Williams was not a slave but a writer savvy enough to realize that the autobiographical genre was the one with the most currency, especially for a black person. Henry Louis Gates Jr., in a lecture delivered at Harvard on December 10, 1999, made a case for rechristening this work a novel. A twentieth-century example of an African American novel passing as an autobiography is, of course, James Weldon Johnson's original 1912 publication of *The Autobiography of an Ex-Coloured Man,* which he published anonymously so as to heighten the generic confusion instigated by the novel's title.
8. Thanks to the literary detective work of Henry Louis Gates Jr. and Bryan C. Sinche, we know something about the books to which Hannah Bond may have had access. See Gates's introduction and appendix C in Crafts, *The Bondwoman's Narrative.*
9. Listed in the catalogue for the 1882 sale of Wheeler's books are *Speeches of William Wilberforce and Others, in 1789, on the Abolition of the Slave Trade* (London, n.d.), and H. W. Beecher, *Star Papers, or Experiences of Art and Nature* (New York, 1855); appendix C in Crafts, *The Bondwoman's Narrative.*
10. Catherine Grace Frances Gore, *The Banker's Wife; or, Court and City: A Novel* (New York: Harper, 1848); and Elizabeth Caroline Gray, *The Gambler's Wife: A Novel* (Philadelphia: T. B. Peterson, 1850). Both of these works appear in appendix C in Crafts, *The Bondwoman's Narrative,* 327.
11. Appendix C in Crafts, *The Bondwoman's Narrative,* 327.
12. Film theorists have productively explored the multilayered reciprocity of genre and audience. See Thomas Schatz, "The Structural Influence: New Directions in Film Genre Studies," and Robin Wood, "Ideology, Genre, Auteur," both in *Film Genre Reader III,* ed. Barry Keith Grant (Austin: University of Texas Press, 2003), 92–102, 60–74.
13. Literary "sampling" is common among African American writers and should be distinguished from Henry Louis Gates Jr.'s concept of "pastiche," discussed in *Signifying Monkey* (New York: Oxford, 1988). See my essay "To Be Continued: Double Identity, Multiplicity and Antigenealogy as Narrative Strategies in Pauline Hopkins' Magazine Fiction," *Callaloo* 22.2 (1999): 483–98, for further discussion of literary sampling.
14. For a detailed analysis of the antebellum literary marketplace, see chapter 1 in my *Truth Stranger Than Fiction* (New York: Palgrave, 2002), as well as Karen

Sanchez-Eppler's *Touching Liberty: Abolition, Feminism, and the Politics of the Body* (Berkeley: University of California Press, 1993).

15. Numerous scholars have remarked on and developed the rhetorical, aesthetic, and political ties to sentimentalism of the slave narrative. In this particular case, see the textual notes for *The Bondwoman's Narrative:* "With the marriage of Lindendale's master, the narrative switches from the style suggestive of the slave narrative and the sentimental novel to a text heavily influenced by gothic patterns and themes. Conventions of the sentimental novel reappear throughout the novel, especially at its denouement." Crafts, *The Bondwoman's Narrative,* 244. Subsequent quotations are cited parenthetically in the text.
16. Humanitarian realism emphasizes suffering—physical, mental, and spiritual—so as to encourage social change in readers. For a detailed discussion of this term and its bearing on the relationship between African American and Anglo-American literature, see my essay "Documenting the Real," in *The Oxford History of the Novel in English,* vol. 6: *The American Novel, 1870–1940,* ed. Priscilla Wald and Michael A. Elliott (Oxford: Oxford University Press, 2014), 103–44.
17. The historical connection between John Hill Wheeler and Jane Johnson was made by William Andrews and reported by Henry Louis Gates Jr. in his introduction to *The Bondwoman's Narrative,* xliv. It has been further documented by Gregg Hecimovich; see "Professor Says He Has Solved a Mystery."
18. William Still, *The Underground Railroad* (Philadelphia: Porter and Coates, 1872).
19. In "Eaten Alive: Slavery and Celebrity in Antebellum America," *ELH* 61.1 (Spring 1994): 159–87, Michael Newbury argues that slavery and celebrity share the same model of labor. His analysis turns on the realization that both the slave and the celebrity are embodied forms of property.
20. Authorship was a public enterprise requiring full and unmolested citizenship, as the advertisement from *The Liberator* demonstrates: "Passmore Williamson in Moyamensing Jail. JUST RELEASED A Fine Portrait representing this Martyr in the cause of Freedom, Truth and Justice (versus Law), taken from life, to the jail in which he has been Imprisoned by Judge Kane." In addition to the historical examples discussed here, Bond provides internal evidence concerning her knowledge of the impact of publication. See her discussion of Byron's sudden fame with the publication of *Don Juan* in Crafts, *A Bondwoman's Narrative,* 213.
21. See Hollis Robbins's insights into Bond's borrowings from Dickens in "A Note on Crafts's Literary Influences," in Crafts, *The Bondwoman's Narrative,* 331–32.
22. Ann Fabian, quoted in Henry Louis Gates Jr.'s introduction to Crafts, *The Bondwoman's Narrative,* finds in the novel "all the clumsy plot structures, changing tenses, impossible coincidences, and heterogeneous elements of the best" of domestic fiction (xxvi).
23. Although we do have *The Curse of Caste; or, The Slave Bride: A Rediscovered African American Novel by Julia C. Collins,* an example of an 1856 African American serial novel discovered by William Andrews and Mitch Kachun (New York: Oxford University Press, 2006), it seems unlikely that Bond was planning on actually publishing the novel in installments (or at all).
24. It seems likely that Wheeler would have subscribed to *The Southern Literary Messenger,* which published Poe. Gates and Robbins point out that Poe's source is Horace Walpole's *Castle of Otranto* (1765). Crafts, *The Bondwoman's Narrative,* 245.

25. For declarations about marriage and romance as privileges of the free, see ibid., lxiii, 120, 131, 206–7. For a fascinating analysis of Hannah's refusal to marry, see Christopher Castiglia, "'I Found a Life of Freedom All My Fancy Had Pictured It to Be': Hannah Crafts's Visual Speculation and the Inner Life of Slavery," in *In Search of Hannah Crafts: Critical Essays on "The Bondwoman's Narrative,"* ed. Henry Louis Gates Jr. and Hollis Robbins (New York: Basic Books, 2004), 231–54.
26. See Priscilla Wald, "Hannah crafts," in Gates and Robbins, *In Search of Hannah Crafts*, 213–229, for a discussion of Crafts's use of the ghost story and its reflection on the history of American slavery.
27. For a detailed and fascinating look at the few figures who were relatively free of the racism that crippled the movement, see John Stauffer, *The Black Hearts of Men* (Cambridge: Harvard University Press, 2002).
28. Asking her readers to "excuse deficiencies in consideration of circumstances," Jacobs makes it clear that she is the sole support of herself and her family, explaining, "Since I have been at the North, it has been necessary for me to work diligently for my own support, and the education of my children." Harriet A. Jacobs, *Incidents in the Life of a Slave Girl*, ed. Jean Fagan Yellin (Cambridge: Harvard University Press 1987), 1.
29. I am indebted for this insight to Priscilla Wald's "Hannah crafts."
30. For a discussion of "the unvarnished truth" as a distinctive trope in mid-nineteenth-century literature, see Ann Fabian, *The Unvarnished Truth: Personal Narratives in Nineteenth-Century America* (Berkeley: University of California Press, 2000).
31. Harriet Jacobs famously told Harriet Beecher Stowe that her book "needed no romance" to succeed; she found a publisher without Stowe's help. Thanks in part to the support of the prominent abolitionist and author Lydia Maria Childs, Jacobs's *Incidents in the Life of a Slave Girl* was published but did not do well despite its connection to Childs. Jacobs fared somewhat better than Harriet Wilson had, but authorship never was the boon for which she had hoped. Thanks to the careful research and literary sleuthing of P. Gabrelle Foreman and Reginald Pitts, we now know that Wilson ended up making a living as a spiritualist in Boston. See Harriet Wilson, *Our Nig*, ed. P. Gabrielle Foreman and Reginald H. Pitts (New York: Penguin, 2004), xxv. R. J. Ellis, in *Harriet Wilson's Our Nig: A Cultural Biography of a "Two-Story" African American Novel* (Amsterdam: Rodopi, 2003), 15–16, has an extended passage on the double meanings of the novel's reference to a "two-story white house" in its subtitle.
32. Add to the example of Wilson the several others we have, including Phillis Wheatley and James Williams, and it would seem clear that African American authorship was limited to autobiography. See chapter 2 of my *Truth Stranger Than Fiction* for further discussion of this fact. For additional discussion of genre in regard to market, see P. Gabrielle Foreman, "Recovered Autobiographies and the Marketplace: *Our Nig's* Generic Genealogies and Harriet Wilson's Entrepreneurial Enterprise," in *Harriet Wilson's New England*, ed. JerriAnn Boggis, Eve Allegra Raimon, and Barbara White (Durham: University of New Hampshire Press, 2007), 123–38.
33. Joyce Wansley, "With the Discovery of *Our Nig*, Henry Gates Becomes the Sherlock Holmes of Black Studies," *People*, September 12, 1983.
34. Established by Boston publishers Ticknor and Fields, and linked to the *Atlantic*

Monthly, the "blue and gold" series published titles that proved to be foundational for what would become the canonical authors of American literature. See Michael Winship, *American Literary Publishing in the Mid-Nineteenth Century: The Business of Ticknor and Fields* (Cambridge: Cambridge University Press, 2003), for the definitive account of this series and its place in American literary history.

35. Now out of print, the collection gave rise to the robust presence of African American women's writing on syllabi and subsequently as subject matter for dissertations, book chapters, and full-length monographs as well as a major digital archive hosted by the Schomburg Center for Research in Black Culture at the New York Public Library.
36. Here I am repurposing Priscilla Wald's pun on Hannah Crafts's name in her essay "Hannah crafts."
37. Henry Lewis Gates Jr., interview by author, June 4, 2007.
38. Ibid.
39. Barbara White, "Afterword: New Information on Harriet Wilson and the Bellmont Family," in Harriet Wilson, *Our Nig*, ed. Henry Louis Gates Jr., 3rd ed. (New York: Vintage, 2002), iii–lvi. See also Eric Gardner, *Unexpected Places: Relocating Nineteenth-Century African American Literature* (Jackson: University of Mississippi Press, 2009).
40. Thanks to the work of P. Gabrielle Foreman and Reginald H. Pitts, we now know that after her literary eclipse, Wilson created a "second story" in which she reinvented herself as a medium and had a successful business in Boston. See Wilson, *Our Nig*, ed. Foreman and Pitts.
41. Henry Lewis Gates Jr., interview by author, June 5, 2007.
42. Ira Berlin, review of *The Bondwoman's Narrative*, ed. Henry Lewis Gates Jr., *Washington Post Book World*, June 23, 2002, 12.
43. Frances Smith Foster, *Written by Herself: Literary Production by African American Women, 1746–1892* (Bloomington: Indiana University Press, 1993), 18.

4. Testimony (The Edition Reimagined)

1. John Bryant provides an excellent overview of this history and its philosophical consequences in "The Textual Debate," chapter 1 of *The Fluid Text: A Theory of Revision and Editing for Book and Screen* (Ann Arbor: University of Michigan Press, 2002). Dubbing texts either "intentional" or "social," according to the editorial approach taken in preparing them for publication, Bryant carefully explains how deeply the editorial approach defines a text. His view, that all texts are fluid—fixed only by virtue of historical and technological limitations—concurs with mine.
2. Jerome McGann, *The Scholar's Art: Literary Studies in a Managed World* (Chicago: University of Chicago Press, 2006), 130.
3. My notion of editions as palimpsests has been strongly influenced by Gérard Genette's book of the same name, *Palimpsests: Literature in the Second Degree*, trans. Channa Newman and Claude Doubinsky (Lincoln: University of Nebraska Press, 1997). For background on Longfellow and his use of editions, see William Charvat, *The Profession of Authorship in America, 1800–1870*, ed. Matthew Bruccoli (New York: Columbia University Press, 1992), 106–55.

4. John Bryant's edition of *Typee* (http://rotunda.upress.virginia.edu) extends a line of thinking that started with Martha Nell Smith's online edition of Emily Dickinson. He articulates much of the theory that went into developing the *Typee* edition in *The Fluid Text.*
5. SocialBook is a project sponsored by The Future of the Book and spearheaded by Bob Stein. Other tools and interfaces that take advantage of the power of reader annotations include the Reading with the Stars feature I have been developing with Reinhard Engles, designer of Highbrow, a deep zoom widget (http://osc.hul.harvard.edu), and Global Huck, a project run by Shelly Fisher Fishkin that will aggregate multiple translations of Mark Twain's masterpiece and capture both critical reception and reader responses.
6. Bob Stein, "Rudimentary Documentation 3.4," http://livemargin.com.
7. In their description and analysis of the recovered William Gibson text "Agrippa," Matthew Kirschenbaum and his colleagues present the exciting conditions of the text which are designed to vanish upon first reading. The challenge Gibson's electronic text poses to traditional reading and scholarly practices bears importantly on the changing nature of the edition, which is the subject of this chapter. Matthew G. Kirschenbaum with Doug Reside and Alan Liu, "No Round Trip: Two New Primary Sources for 'Agrippa,'" http://agrippa.english.ucsb.edu.
8. In *Palimpsests,* Genette uses the term "open structuralism" to account for what he calls the textual transcendence of literary works.
9. Kirschenbaum, Reside, and Liu, "No Round Trip." Robert Darnton first freed the book from the oversimplified notions of its context in his breakthrough article "What Is the History of Books?" *Daedalus* 111.3 (1982): 65–83; Bryant's *Fluid Text* takes up this work with gusto. Ultimately, Bryant's concern is to restore and replenish a critical concept of creativity—with regard to both the artist and the reader/critic.
10. In the nineteenth century, simultaneous publication was a way to protect an author's claim to copyright. Melville, for instance, entrusted his manuscript of *Typee* to his brother, who took it across the ocean and had it published in England to ensure that Melville would profit from its publication.
11. Melissa J. Homestead, "The Publishing History of Augusta Jane Evans's Confederate Novel *Macaria:* Unwriting Some Lost Cause Myths," *Mississippi Quarterly: The Journal of Southern Cultures* 28.3–4 (2005): 665–702. Homestead found "circumstantial evidence that Evans was sending sheets to [the New York publisher] Derby beginning in late 1863, and while Lippincott (who took the work on for Derby) announced an edition as in press, the edition that actually hit the market first was John Bradburn's, which did *not* derive from those sheets, but from a complete copy of the Confederate first edition he had gotten his hands on. Bradburn created stereotype plates, and Carleton acquired these plates, making this 'unauthorized' wartime edition into the 'authorized' and official postwar edition (there was no stereotype foundry in the South in late 1863, and besides, the edition is in cramped double columns)." Homestead, e-mail communication with the author, March 7, 2009.
12. I owe a special debt of gratitude to Melissa Homestead for sharing her research on Evans and *Macaria* in particular with me, as well as her chapter on Evans in her book *American Women Authors and Literary Property, 1822–1869* (New York:

Cambridge University Press, 2005). The Boston Athenaeum granted me access to their superb collection of Southern periodicals and supported my work during the summer of 2006 with kindness and diligence.

13. N. Katherine Hayles, *Electronic Literature: New Horizons for the Literary* (Notre Dame: University of Notre Dame Press, 2008), 162–63.
14. Clifford Geertz, "Deep Play: Notes on the Balinese Cockfight," in *The Interpretation of Cultures* (New York: Basic Books, 1973), 412–53. In my turn to Geertz, I am extending an insight John Bryant develops regarding authorship in the production of editions (*Fluid Text,* 54).
15. According to Melissa Homestead, there were two 1864 Confederate editions; an 1864 New York edition; an 1864 London edition, published by Saunders & Otley; an edition the New York publisher George Carleton brought out, with plates bought from John Bradburn so the book could be reissued when Evans's next novel, *St. Elmo,* came out in 1867–68; and the revised 1896 edition (Homestead e-mail). In addition to these, I have found references to a London edition of the 1890s as well as another English edition in 1910: *Macaria; Or, Altars of Sacrifice* (London: W. Nicholson, 1890s), 378 pages, plate, 19 cm; and *Macaria* (London: G. Routledge, 1910), 380 pages, [1] leaf of plates, ill., 19 cm. Although catalogue entries such as these can be erroneous, it is worth noting that the 1910 copy has more pages but the same page size (19 cm) as the earlier one.
16. As Rebecca Grant Sexton notes, "the fact . . . that [Nina] Baym would use [Evans's] novels to illustrate the rise and fall of the domestic novel in America is indicative of [her] popularity and importance in nineteenth-century literature." Rebecca Grant Sexton, ed., *A Southern Woman of Letters: The Correspondence of Augusta Jane Evans Wilson* (Columbia: University of South Carolina Press, 2002), xxvii.
17. Elizabeth Moss, *Domestic Novelists in the Old South* (Baton Rouge: Louisiana State University Press, 1992), 3. (Moss identifies Irene Huntingdon, the protagonist of *Macaria,* as a journalist, but this is likely a mistaken reference to the title character of *Beulah,* who is a journalist.)
18. Ibid., 26.
19. All of Evans's novels remained in print—and sold—throughout her lifetime and beyond. As a point of comparison, Herman Melville's most popular novel, *Typee,* remained in print throughout his lifetime while his other novels did not. John Bryant tracks Melville's reactions, responses, and interventions throughout *The Fluid Text;* his discussion of Melville's revisions of the scene in which Tommo takes a bath (53–63) is especially helpful in showing Melville's efforts to address multiple readerships and their concerns.
20. Franco Moretti, *Graphs, Maps, Trees: Abstract Models for Literary History* (London: Verso, 2005), 2.
21. William Perry Fidler, *Augusta Evans Wilson, 1835–1909: A Biography* (Birmingham: University of Alabama Press, 1951), 27, 40–41.
22. According to Fidler, several prominent Mobilians have been mentioned as the "'angel' of *Inez,* but the donor was probably Augustus Howard, the novelist's uncle and namesake" (ibid., 45). Melissa Homestead has since contested the claim that the novel's publication was subsidized. Homestead, "Publishing History," 670n12.

23. Fidler, *Augusta Evans Wilson,* 40–44.
24. Homestead recognizes the effort to secure the delicate balance between the North and the South according to what David Blight has termed "reconciliation logic" in the revised narrative of *Macaria*'s publication history. Building on the narrativizing tendency she establishes, I turn to the literary term that best describes the generic reading practices her study suggests we use. David W. Blight, *Race and Reunion: The Civil War in American Memory* (Cambridge: Harvard University Press, 2001).
25. Fidler, *Augusta Evans Wilson,* 60.
26. Jones later died on the Gettysburg battlefield.
27. Fidler, *Augusta Evans Wilson,* 68; William L. G. Smith, *Life at the South or Uncle Tom's Cabin as It Is* (Buffalo: G. H. Derby & Co., 1852).
28. Fidler, *Augusta Evans Wilson,* 68–69, 75.
29. William Smith, ed., *Dictionary of Greek and Roman Mythology* (Boston: Little, Brown, 1849), 2:1090. This was likely the same source that Evans herself used to refresh her memory.
30. William Charvat, *Literary Publishing in America, 1790–1850* (Amherst: University of Massachusetts Press, 1993).
31. Augusta Jane Evans, "Northern Literature," *Mobile Daily Advertiser,* October 10, 1859.
32. Quoted in Fidler, *Augusta Evans Wilson,* 77.
33. Evans, "Northern Literature."
34. Fidler, *Augusta Evans Wilson,* 70.
35. Evans, "Northern Literature."
36. Clifford Geertz, "A Strange Romance: Anthropology and Literature," *Profession* 1 (2003): 28–36. In defining and explaining anthropological practices, Geertz finds his own discipline to be, in the end, "rather like literature, actually" (29).
37. General G. H. Thomas called it "contraband and dangerous" and saw to its burning in his Union camp in Tennessee. Fidler, *Augusta Evans Wilson,* 107.
38. Literary historians from Fred Patee to Nina Baym and beyond agree on the importance of Evans's work in terms of both its popularity and its impact. *Beulah, Macaria,* and *St. Elmo* are all purported to have been best-sellers; *St. Elmo* is said to have been second in popularity only to *Uncle Tom's Cabin.* Standard editions of Evans's first seven novels were issued in 1887 and again in 1897 with the same plates by the New York publisher Dillingham. Fidler, *Augusta Evans Wilson,* 230. See also Susan S. Williams, *Reclaiming Authorship: Literary Women in America, 1850–1900* (Philadelphia: University of Pennsylvania Press, 2006), 17.
39. Suzanne Ashworth, in "Reading Mind, Reading Body: Augusta Jane Evans' *Beulah* and the Physiology of Reading," in *Reading Women: Literary Figures and Cultural Icons from the Victorian Age to the Present,* ed. Janet Badia and Jennifer Phegley (Toronto: University of Toronto Press, 2005), 77–104, identifies Evans's conception of Southern womanhood as describing another race entirely. As intriguing as I find this formulation, it appears at odds with the more compelling aspects of her argument regarding Evans's popularity: "*Beulah* spoke to audiences and ideologies that exceeded Dixie's borders. . . . [I]t's a literary artifact that resounds with national import: twenty-two thousand copies of *Beulah* were printed in the first nine months after its release, and its plot, style, and themes mirror those of *St. Elmo* (1867), the clear-cut blockbuster Evans would publish eight years later" (79).

40. Moss, *Domestic Novelists*, 179.
41. Here again, Evans finds common ground with Alcott, Stowe, and Whitman.
42. Moss, *Domestic Novelists*, 181. Homestead has also debunked the claims that there were two Southern edition of *Macaria* (1863 and 1864) and that its covers and binding were made of wallpaper as simply further romanticizing elements of Evans as a Southern publishing legend. Homestead, "Publishing History," 675–76.
43. Fidler, *Augusta Evans Wilson*, 75, 45.
44. Alice Fahs, *The Imagined Civil War: Popular Literature of the North and South, 1861–1865* (Chapel Hill: University of North Carolina Press, 2001), 116. Fahs concludes, "Increasingly during the war popular literature insisted on a democratization of the nation itself" (116).
45. See especially *Aunt Phillis's Cabin* (1852) and *Life at the South or Uncle Tom's Cabin as It Is* (1852). See http://utc.iath.virginia.edu for examples of the commercial presence of the novel from its first publication through the early twentieth century.
46. Advertisement, *Mobile Daily Register*, May 4, 1864.
47. In her paper "Soldiers, Readers, and the Reception of Victor Hugo's *Les Misérables* in Civil War America," presented at the American Literature Association annual conference, San Francisco, May 25, 2012, Vanessa Steinroetter tracks the popularity of Hugo's novel among readers during the Civil War. The article version of the ALA paper is forthcoming as "Soldiers, Readers, and the Reception of Victor Hugo's *Les Misérables* in Civil War America," in the journal *Reception: Texts, Readers, Audiences, History*.
48. Augusta Jane Evans. *Macaria; Or, Altars of Sacrifice*, ed. Drew Gilpin Faust (Baton Rouge: Louisiana University Press, 1992), 5. Subsequent quotations from this edition are cited parenthetically in the text.
49. Evans, "Northern Literature."
50. Fidler, *Augusta Evans Wilson*, 4.
51. See http://eliotswasteland.tripod.com for a hypertext version of Eliot's poem.
52. Sexton, *A Southern Woman of Letters*, 104.
53. Elizabeth Moss's chapter on Evans in *Domestic Novelists in the Old South* is especially helpful in the way it distinguishes Evans from her contemporaries.
54. See the entry for "Macaria" in the online Encyclopedia Mythica, www.pantheon.org.
55. See also Ashworth, "Reading Mind, Reading Body," for a sustained analysis of Evans's view of Southern womanhood through a careful examination of reading as an activity in *Beulah* and as an object of scientific study in the mid-nineteenth century.
56. Important studies of the nineteenth century, including work by Renee Bergland, Laura Dassow Walls, and Eric Wilson, have shown the diverse and cosmopolitan interests of readers during this period. Scientists and humanists had not yet divided themselves into "two cultures" (as C. P. Snow described them in the early twentieth century). What we might treat as cross-disciplinary investigations—as Evans takes up science, law, and Greek mythology—are more properly part of the lingua franca of nineteenth-century public culture.
57. Thomas Hardy's *Two on a Tower* (1882) fruitfully reworks the astronomer as a romantic figure to tell the rather conventional story of "star-crossed" lovers

who share a love of the stars in heaven while they are bound to obey the laws of human culture.

58. Nina Baym, in *American Women of Letters and the Nineteenth-Century Sciences* (New Brunswick: Rutgers University Press, 2004), holds that Irene is neither brilliant nor professional in part because there is no precedent for such a character in the real world. She contrasts her with the novel's other important female character, Electra, who goes to New York and becomes a professional artist. Other contemporary scholars have found Irene's choices disappointing from a feminist perspective—among them Naomi Sofer, in *Making the "America of Art": Cultural Nationalism and Nineteenth-Century Women Writers* (Columbus: Ohio State University Press, 2005), Moss, in *Domesticating Novelists*, and Fahs, in *The Imagined Civil War.*
59. Her *Urania propitia, sive Tabulae Astronomicae mire faciles, vim hypothesium physicarum a Kepplero proditarum complexae; facillimo calculandi compendio, sine ulla Logarithmorum mentione*... (1650), which includes a preface by her husband in which he fully attributes the work to Cunitz, is an astronomical ephemeris based on Kepler's Rudolphine tables. Cunitz believed that "the so-called Danish Tables of Longomontanus" were in error, and "although the Rudolphine Tables of Kepler were more accurate, they were very difficult to calculate and apply" because they used logarithms. See Robert A. Hatch, "The Cuniz Page: A Brief Chronology of the Life of Maria Cunitz," http://web.clas.ufl.edu.
60. Hypatia's prominence was accentuated by the fact that she was both female and pagan in an increasingly Christian environment. She was beaten, murdered, and then mutilated in a church by a group of Christian monks in the spring of 415 C.E. See the entry for Hypatia at http://cosmopolis.com.
61. According to Drew Gilpin Faust's rough assessment, revisions over the editions fall into two main categories: style and historical references. The 1896 edition has fewer erudite references; the ardent pro-South sentiment has also been noticeably muted. Evans, *Macaria*, ed. Faust, xxviii–xxix.
62. Elizabeth Fekete Trubey, "Emancipating the Lettered Slave: Sentiment and Slavery in Augusta Evans's *St. Elmo*," *American Literature* 77.1 (2005): 124.
63. Here I am glossing on James Machor's gloss on Stephen Greenblatt in "Fiction and Informed Reading in Early Nineteenth-Century America," *Nineteenth-Century Literature* 47.3 (1992): 320.
64. Thanks to Erin Hendel for calling this to my attention. Her dissertation, "We the Many Peoples: Literatures of Alternative Nationalisms in the United States, 1820–1900" (University of California, Davis), will include a chapter on *Macaria*, part of which she presented at the American Literature Association annual convention on May 24, 2012.
65. Fidler, *Augusta Evans Wilson*, 126.
66. Evans, *Macaria*, ed. Faust, xxvi.
67. Machor, "Fiction and Informed Reading," 320.
68. Elizabeth Fekete Trubey's discussion of Evans's *St. Elmo* as "a complicated mire of affection and ownership, autonomy and obedience, submission and rebellion" ("Emancipating the Lettered Slave," 124) has been helpful to me in my thinking about this earlier text. In referring to Evans's "inflection" of sentimentalism, for instance, I am building on the thrust of her argument about Southern forms

of sentimentalism as regionalized rather than "translated." *St. Elmo*'s treatment of women and authorship reflect a postwar anxiety absent from *Macaria*, however.

69. James Green, "The Publishing History of Olaudah Equiano's *Interesting Narrative*," *Slavery and Abolition* 16.3 (1995): 362–75.

5. Loss (Authorship Regained)

1. Michel Foucault, *Language, Counter-Memory, Practice: Selected Essays and Interviews*, ed. Donald F. Bouchard (Ithaca: Cornell University Press, 1977), 138.
2. For a detailed explanation of this software and the way it has been developed and implemented, see "About Commentpress" at http://futureofthebook.org. Another open source software program, PressBook, improves on CommentPress by allowing for greater flexibility in layout as well as the inclusion of other media. With PressBook, users can make more choices on a formal level as well as in terms of content.
3. See Jay Rosen, "The People Formerly Known as the Audience," June 27, 2006, and Jay Rosen, "Blogger vs. Journalists Is Over," January 21, 2005, both at http://archive.pressthink.org.
4. The title was supplied by George Lorimer, the editor of the *Saturday Evening Post*. The *Post* published five serialized sections of the book that later bore this title.
5. *A Diary from Dixie, as written by Mary Boykin Chesnut, Wife of James Chesnut, Jr., United States Senator from South Carolina, 1859–1861, and Afterward Aide to Jefferson Davis and a Brigadier General in the Confederate Army*, ed. Isabella D. Martin and Myrta Lockett Avary (New York: Appleton, 1905), hereafter cited parenthetically as *Diary* 1905; *A Diary from Dixie by Mary Boykin Chesnut*, ed. Ben Ames Williams (Boston: Houghton Mifflin, 1949), hereafter cited parenthetically as *Diary* 1949; *Mary Chesnut's Civil War*, ed. C. Vann Woodward (New Haven: Yale University Press, 1981), hereafter cited parenthetically as *MCCW*.
6. Sharon Cameron, *Writing Nature: Henry Thoreau's* Journal (Chicago: University of Chicago Press, 1989), provides an overview of this text's publication history in her introductory chapter, "The *Journal* against *Walden*: A Preliminary Perspective," 3–27. See also Lawrence Buell, *The Environmental Imagination: Thoreau, Nature Writing, and the Formation of American Culture* (Cambridge: Belknap, 1995), especially the chapter "*Walden*'s Environmental Projects," 115–39; H. Daniel Peck, "Unlikely Kindred Spirits: A New Vision of Landscape in the Works of Henry David Thoreau and Asher B. Durand," *American Literary History* 17.4 (2005): 687–713; and William Rossi, "The Journal, Self-Culture, and the Genesis of 'Walking,'" *Thoreau Quarterly* 16.3–4 (1984): 138–55.
7. We could notate the initial "diary" as Diary^0. According to the laws of exponents, anything to the power of zero equals 1. Thus, by representing the initial diary written by Chesnut as Diary^0, I am calling attention to its irreducibility as a whole entity that increases exponentially with each edition.
8. Exponents provide a helpful mechanism for notation in this case as they are designed to help solve problems that involve variables.
9. My initial insight into the transformation of the editor into an author comes

from Leah Price, *The Anthology and the Rise of the Novel* (Cambridge: Cambridge University Press, 2000).

10. Elisabeth Muhlenfeld, *Mary Boykin Chesnut* (Baton Rouge: Louisiana University Press, 1981), 9–11.
11. It might be useful to remind the reader what an integer is and how it figures in this argument. According to Wikipedia: "The integers (from the Latin *integer*, literally 'untouched,' hence 'whole': the word *entire* comes from the same origin, but via French) are formed by the natural numbers including 0 (0, 1, 2, 3, . . .) together with the negatives of the non-zero natural numbers (-1, -2, -3, . . .). Viewed as a subset of the real numbers, they are numbers that can be written without a fractional or decimal component, and fall within the set {. . . -2, -1, 0, 1, 2, . . .}. For example, 65, 7, and -759 are integers; 1.6 and 1½ are not integers."
12. Jerome J. McGann, "Literary Pragmatics and the Editorial Horizon," in *The Textual Condition* (Princeton: Princeton University Press, 1991), 33.
13. Both Muhlenfeld and Woodward treat this problem extensively, so I simply rehearse the difficulties for the sake of readers who may not be familiar with this source material and its history. *The Private Mary Chesnut: The Unpublished Civil War Diaries*, ed. C. Vann Woodward and Elisabeth Muhlenfeld (New York: Oxford University Press, 1984), 1.
14. See Rebecca Steinitz, *Time, Space, and Gender in the Nineteenth-Century British Diary* (New York: Palgrave Macmillan, 2011), for a detailed discussion of the diary as a "profoundly cultural form, highly implicated in the dominant ideologies of its time, rather than simply an individualistic expression of unmediated subjectivity" (6).
15. *The Private Mary Chesnut*, 1.
16. Ibid. 6.
17. Ibid. 6.
18. Alice Fahs, *The Imagined Civil War: Popular Literature of the North and South, 1861–1865* (Chapel Hill: University of North Carolina Press, 2001), 287ff.
19. Quoted in Muhlenfeld, *Mary Boykin Chesnut*, 214.
20. Elisabeth Muhlenfeld, "The Civil War and Authorship," in *The History of Southern Literature*, ed. Louis Rubin et al. (Baton Rouge: Louisiana State University Press, 1985), 184.
21. Ibid., 185.
22. Ibid., 187.
23. Woodward, *MCCW*, xxiv.
24. Melissa Mentzer has constructed a feminist reading of Chesnut's revisions in "Rewriting Herself: Mary Chesnut's Narrative Strategies," *Connecticut Review* 14.1 (Spring 1992): 49–55.
25. N. Katherine Hayles, *Writing Machines* (Cambridge: MIT Press, 2002), 117.
26. Frederick S. Bigelow, *A Short History of the* Saturday Evening Post (New York: Curtis, 1927), 8.
27. According to Jan Cohn, *Creating America: George Horace Lorimer and the* Saturday Evening Post (Pittsburgh: University of Pittsburgh Press, 1989), 46, 59, circulation at the time was somewhere between 500,000 (1903) and 725,000 (1907), and Lorimer was touting the *Post* as "the greatest weekly magazine in the world." Bigelow (*Short History*, 15) remarks that "it crossed the million net paid mark in

1904, the first magazine to do so." Although these figures are contradictory, the magazine clearly had a significant readership. In addition, after an early advertising campaign led by Ayer and Co., during which the *Saturday Evening Post* was sent on a trial basis to doctors' and dentists' offices, we can assume that paid subscription numbers can reflect only a percentage of readers.

28. Bigelow, *Short History*, 12.
29. For a through analysis of the narrative value of the serial form, see my "'To Be Continued': Double Identity, Multiplicity, and Antigenealogy as Narrative Strategies in Pauline Hopkins' Magazine Fiction," *Callaloo* 22.2 (Spring 1999): 483–98; Christopher Looby, "Southworth and Seriality: The Hidden Hand in the *New York Ledger*," *Nineteenth-Century Literature* 59.2 (September 2004): 179–211; and Jennifer DeVere Brody, *Punctuation: Art, Politics, Play* (Durham: Duke University Press 2008).
30. *Saturday Evening Post*, January 28, 1905, 1.
31. This image of Mary with her husband early in the marriage is held by the Granger Collection, New York.
32. Roland Barthes, *Camera Lucida: Reflections on Photography*, trans. Richard Howard (New York: Hill and Wang, 1981), 76.
33. See "The Lists," *New York Times*, October 7, 1905: "The annual announcement of Spring books follows, including those published between Feb 1 and July 1. The Titles have been carefully arranged and classified so as to make the lists as useful as possible to intending purchasers of books."
34. Grant Overton, *Portrait of a Publisher* (New York: D. Appleton, 1925), 5.
35. Ibid., 6.
36. Ibid., 19–20.
37. Appleton's successes were not limited to discovering new authors; he ushered in an innovative new form to please popular tastes and accommodate a modest budget. *Picturesque America*, edited by William Cullen Byrant, offered readers the serialized book in pamphlet form. Brought out in twenty-page segments and then bound as a volume, *Picturesque America* offered readers heavily illustrated historical content in small, affordable pieces. Appleton was also a pioneer in cheap editions and paperbacks. His Town and Country Library published Conrad, among others.
38. Overton, *Portrait*, 11.
39. Ibid., 20–21.
40. Muhlenfeld, *Mary Boykin Chesnut*, 6.
41. Avary followed the 1905 publication of *A Diary from Dixie* with *Dixie after the War: Eyewitness Accounts of Reconstruction* in 1906.
42. Anthony Grafton, *The Footnote: A Curious History* (Cambridge: Harvard University Press, 1999), 5.
43. Dodd penned a textbook, *The Cotton Kingdom: A Chronicle of the Old South*, published by Yale University Press in 1919, as well as a biography of Jefferson Davies (Philadelphia: G. W. Jacobs, 1907) and *Expansion and Conflict: A History of the United States* (Boston: Houghton Mifflin, 1915).
44. "'Mrs. Chesnut's Diary': A Chronicle of Southern Life by the Wife of a Confederate Statesman and Soldier," *New York Times Book Review*, April 22, 1905, 22.
45. "Books and Authors," *New York Times Book Review*, April 22, 1905, 22.
46. "Mrs. Chesnut's Diary," 22.

47. Both C. Vann Woodward and Chesnut's biographer Elisabeth Muhlenfeld agree that Chesnut's work in fiction helped her develop as a writer.
48. In "The Masterpiece That Became a Hoax" (*New York Times*, April 26, 1981), Kenneth Lynn compares the 1880s version of the Diary to "the soggily nostalgic stories that Thomas Nelson Page began to publish in the 80's" and "to Thomas Dixon's *The Clansman* (1905) with its nightmarish vision of savage blacks running amok. . . . Both by what she left out of her simulated diary and by what she put into it, Mary Chesnut defined her agreement with the aims of this disgraceful literary movement."
49. Michael Levenson, in *A Genealogy of Modernism: A Study of English Literary Doctrine, 1908–1922* (Cambridge: Cambridge University Press, 1984), identifies consciousness and subjectivist perspective as one pole of modernism. For a discussion of the relationship between stream of consciousness and first-person narration, see Dorrit Cohn, *Transparent Minds: Narrative Modes for Presenting Consciousness* (Princeton: Princeton University Press, 1978).
50. Also on the best-seller list in 1947 was Frank Yerby's *The Vixens,* John Steinbeck's *The Wayward Bus,* and Sinclair Lewis's *Kingsblood Royal.*
51. According to Williams's introduction, the 1905 edition contained about 150,000 words; the manuscript copy of the original Diary is nearly 400,000 words. The 1949 edition is approximately 300,000 (*Diary* 1949, xxiii–xxiv).
52. See my *Truth Stranger Than Fiction: Race, Realism, and the U.S. Literary Marketplace* (New York: Palgrave, 2002), xv, 5, 21–27, 29, 55–60, 115.
53. *Diary* 1949, 139.
54. Hayden White, *Metahistory: The Historical Imagination in Nineteenth-Century Europe* (Baltimore: Johns Hopkins University Press, 1973).
55. I owe much to Virginia Jackson's discussion of Emily Dickinson's work as formally unclassifiable and materially unpublished for helping me further my own thinking about Chesnut. Virginia Jackson, *Dickinson's Misery: A Theory of Lyric Reading* (Princeton: Princeton University Press, 2005).
56. Blakey Vermeule, "Gossip and Literary Narrative," *Philosophy and Literature* 30.1 (April 2006): 104, 106–7.
57. Patricia Meyer Spacks, *Gossip* (New York: Knopf, 1985), 3, 5.
58. Julia Stern, *Mary Chesnut's Unfinished Epic* (Chicago: University of Chicago Press, 2009).
59. My concept of the remnant is derived from Giorgio Agamben's *Remnants of Auschwitz: The Witness and the Archive,* trans. Daniel Heller-Roazen (New York: Zone Books, 2002).
60. I am indebted to Todd Hagstette at the University of South Carolina for his faithful transcription of "The Bright Side of Richmond" and to Thomas Brown of the University of South Carolina history department, a fellow Chesnut scholar, for putting me together with Hagstette. Not only did Hagstette produce a professional transcription, but he also was an interesting interlocutor, posing questions and making suggestions as I developed this stage of my analysis. His knowledge of South Carolina history and Southern literature, and his overall good judgment, were essential. As Hagstette explained: "The numbering at the top of the pages is all printed by M.B.C. Towards the end of the document she frequently changes original page numbers to fit into her new organization for

this document. The 'framing' that I make note of on the first page is the norm for her page numbering style. Afterwards, I take note of any variations in it. So, after page 1, if the number is unbracketed it means that the number appears with the framing and there is nothing unusual about its appearance." E-mail communication, May 29, 2008. I left a copy of the transcription made by Hagstette on deposit at the Ernest F. Hollings Special Collections Library at the University of South Carolina for future researchers to consult; it differs in considerable ways from the version published in Woodward, *MCCW*, 528–47.

61. Here I compare "The Bright Side of Richmond" to another discrete project found in the archives. Prompted by W. W. Butler, who was calling for biographical sketches of prominent men, Chesnut prepared a brief sketch of her husband, James Chesnut. Unlike in "The Bright Side of Richmond," however, this manuscript's pages are not numbered by Chesnut, a process she appears to have used only in the final phases of revision.
62. Brody, *Punctuation*, 6.
63. James Wood Davidson, *The Living Writers of the South* (New York: Carleton, 1869), 313.
64. Agamben, *Remnants of Auschwitz*, 158.
65. Jackson, *Dickinson's Misery.*
66. See the preface to Myrta Avary, *A Virginia Girl during the Civil War*, Holly M. Kent's paper "'The Fair Readers of My Country': Women's Literature in *The Genius of Universal Emancipation*, 1821–1831," delivered at the Society for Historians of the Early American Republic conference in July 2007, identifies the prevalence of this genre of historiography.
67. Agamben, *Remnants of Auschwitz*, 142.

Epilogue

1. Miranda Maher, email communication regarding her "Manipulated Books" Web exhibit, February 4, 2014. The exhibit, originally at http://miranda-maher.com, is no longer online.
2. In a June 13, 2011, talk, "Track Changes," presented at the Digital Humanities Summer Institute in Victoria, British Columbia, Matthew Kirschenbaum elaborated on how all digital documents are both data and metadata.
3. Walter Benjamin, "Theses on the Philosophy of History," in *Illuminations*, ed. Hannah Arendt, trans. Harry Zohn (New York: Schocken, 1968), 253–64, 261.
4. Ibid., 255.
5. The fulcrum of the move toward a more inclusive literary history in and of the United States was the publication of the *Heath Anthology*. According to the book's website: "When the Heath, as it has come to be called, first came out in 1989 it was both a symbol and a tool. It symbolized the desire among many teachers, critics, and students to study the full range of the literatures produced in America rather than the very limited number of works that had come to be known as the 'literary canon.' And it provided a tool, in the form of a diverse collection of literary works, for broadening our view of the authors and texts worth reading and thinking about. The Heath challenged all of us to respond to earlier

movements for social change that had asked of our classrooms, our curricula, our textbooks questions like 'where are the minorities?' 'where are the women?' And once these voices began to be heard, new questions arose, like 'what differences did difference make?' and 'how would our understanding of all American culture be transformed by their inclusion in the cultural conversation'?" "Heath Orientation," www.cengage.com.

6. Giorgio Agamben, *Remnants of Auschwitz: The Witness and the Archive*, trans. Daniel Heller-Roazen (New York: Zone Books, 2002), 145.
7. This characterization of the offline archive owes much to the call for papers for a special session convened by the American Literature Division at MLA 2009 by Anna Brickhouse.
8. Here I am "repurposing" observations that Ravit Reichman made regarding property for the insight her remarks provide on the archive: "As a condition, it aims to freeze time and produce nostalgia, while as a dynamic and unpredictable process, it can inaugurate a narrative that resists the possibility of stasis and releases an emotional current not of nostalgia but of grief—and ultimately, indebtedness." Ravit Reichman, "Mourning, Owning, Owing," *American Imago* 64. 3 (2007): 433.
9. The editor or editors, in turn, work together with information technologists and designers. Upon review, this configuration looks very much like Darnton's publication circuit.
10. Agamben, *Remnants of Auschwitz*, 148.
11. Diana Coole and Samantha Frost, "Introducing the New Materialisms," in *New Materialisms: Ontology, Agency, and Politics*, ed. Diana Coole and Samantha Frost (Durham: Duke University Press, 2010), 9.
12. N. Katherine Hayles, *How We Became Posthuman* (Chicago: University of Chicago Press 1999), 47.
13. *PMLA* published a cluster of articles on the Whitman online archive which work through some of the conceptual issues I am focusing on here, though they concentrate primarily on the form and idea of the database as it pertains to the formation of knowledge. *PMLA* 122.5 (October 2007): 1577–1610.
14. Walt Whitman, *Specimen Days*, in *Leaves of Grass: Comprehensive Reader's Edition*, ed. Harold W. Blodgett and Sculley Bradley (New York: New York University Press, 1965).
15. Lambasted for its argument against women's literature, Ann Douglas's *Feminization of American Culture* (New York: Farrar, Straus and Giroux, 1998) is an interesting example of the anxieties recovered texts can unleash. Pitting Melville against women writers of his period, Douglas found that women lacked the aesthetic sine qua non of modernism: ambiguity.
16. Amy Earhart explores the downside of Web-based textual production, exposing the return of canonical dominance due to the de facto cultural gatekeeping created by granting agencies and other funders. She produces statistics that show an alarming lack of work by women and writers of color. Amy Earhart, "Can Information Be Unfettered? Race and the New Digital Humanities Canon," in *Debates in the Digital Humanities*, ed. Matthew K. Gold (Minneapolis: University of Minnesota Press, 2012), 309–19.
17. Kirschenbaum, "Track Changes."
18. According to Wikipedia: "Participatory culture is a neologism in reference of,

but opposite to a Consumer culture—in other words a culture in which private persons (the public) do not act as consumers only, but also as contributors or producers (prosumers). The term is most often applied to the production or creation of some type of published media. Recent advances in technologies (mostly personal computers and the Internet) have enabled private persons to create and publish such media, usually through the Internet. This new culture as it relates to the Internet has been described as Web 2.0. In participatory culture 'young people creatively respond to a plethora of electronic signals and cultural commodities in ways that surprise their makers, finding meanings and identities never meant to be there and defying simple nostrums that bewail the manipulation or passivity of 'consumers'" [*sic*]. Citing Paul Willis, "Foot Soldiers of Modernity: The Dialectics of Cultural Consumption and the 21st-Century School," *Harvard Educational Review* 73.3 (2003): 392.

19. Strawberry Saroyan, "Amanda Hocking, Storyseller," *New York Times Magazine*, June 19, 2011, 26.
20. Benjamin, "Theses on the Philosophy of History," 263.
21. Ibid., 255.
22. Publications for lay readers such as *The Shallows* (New York: Norton, 2010) by Nicholas Carr, and *The Information* (New York: Pantheon, 2011) by James Glieck, as well as others that are more academic, such as Ann Blair's *Too Much to Know: Managing Scholarly Information before the Modern Age* (New Haven: Yale University Press, 2010), show the ongoing nature of the debate over the results of information overload, both past and present.

Index

AUGUSTA ROHRBACH was born and raised in New York City, where she attended the High School of Art and Design. She received a B.A. from the Seminar College at the New School for Social Research and a Ph.D. from Columbia University. She has been the recipient of a Bunting Fellowship and then was a jointly appointed fellow at the Radcliffe Institute for Advanced Study and the W. E. B. Du Bois Research Institute at Harvard University. Her first book was *Truth Stranger Than Fiction: Race, Realism, and the U.S. Literary Marketplace* (2002). She lives in Cambridge, Mass.